This book is dedicated to my dear wife Becky. It is her patience and heart for God that has allowed me to pursue my Lord in the wilderness.

Photos by S R Dare

Cover Photo - *Paths Less Taken*

Contents Photo - *Tree of Truth*

Photo pg. 30 - *God's Majesty*

Photo pg. 86 - *A Lamp for my Feet*

Photo pg. 141 - *Deep Calls to Deep*

CONTENTS

But blessed is the one who trusts in the Lord, whose confidence is in him.
They will be like a tree planted by the water that sends out its roots by the
stream. Jeremiah 17:7-8 NIV

Forward

What an honor is has been to journey with Shannon in the compilation of these devotionals. I love Shannon's writing style. I feel like we are sitting at the kitchen table over coffee or tea as Shannon shares a story. The beauty comes as his words bring the sights, sounds, and all our senses alive.

We can hear the roar of the falls and taste the breeze as it moves across the grass and rustles our clothes. We feel the path beneath our feet and the lilt of laughter that carries us along. In mystery and wonder we are ready to hear the Spirit - He speaks. Like the ancient text says, "Go out and stand on the mountain before the LORD. Behold, the LORD is about to pass by." And a great and mighty wind tore into the mountains and shattered the rocks before the LORD, but the LORD was not in the wind. After the wind there was an earthquake, but the LORD was not in the earthquake. After the earthquake there was a fire, but the LORD was not in the fire. And after the fire came a still, small voice...." God whispers our name. He calls to our heart. He reaches for our hand and leads us along His path.

If you are ready for the voice of God in your life, then you are ready for this devotional experience. Come!

Keith Wooden

Introduction

As men, we are called to a special relationship with God. Like Adam walking and talking with Him in the garden, we too are invited to a personal and intimate relationship with the Lord. Mankind is fearfully and wonderfully made in His image and carries the authority of dominion over the earth, and the responsibility of leadership in His Kingdom. Within that calling, we have the privilege of being instruments of love and encouragement to those God brings into our lives.

To accomplish this calling, we must keep our eyes fixed on Jesus, surrendering our agenda for the purposeful will of our Creator. This singular focus on our Amazing Father results in peace beyond understanding.

As the writer of Hebrews put it, *"Let us hold unswervingly to the hope we profess, for He who promised is faithful. And let us consider how we may spur one another on toward love and good deeds."* (Hebrews 10:23-24 NIV)

There is much to be thankful for through the sacrifice of Jesus on the cross. Let us spur one another on toward love and good deeds, giving thanks and praise to our faithful Father. *"Now to the King eternal, immortal, invisible, the only God, be honor and glory for ever and ever. Amen."* (I Timothy 1:17 NIV)

The events described in these devotions are largely true. Though poetic license has been liberally used, things happened much like they are described.

-Day 1-

Solitude in the Forest
Life in the Stillness

Shimmering rays of sun drenched the forest with a warm glow as I eased myself down onto the leaf-cluttered ground. Little smidgeons of rosehip, missed when clearing a place to sit, clung to my clothing. As I chastised them with my bare fingers it dislocated some of the leaves piled around sending a loud rustling noise into the woods. Settling in I leaned against a log and became still.

All morning I had been walking through the woods looking for new sights and enjoying the solitude of the area. The broken woodlots of central Indiana provide great habitat for all manner of creatures native to the area. Most people miss the inhabitants of the woods and the amazing lives they live because they never stop to watch and listen.

Throughout the morning I enjoyed the smells of fall and took in the vivid colors of the season. During my "walk-about" I managed to flush two woodcocks (precocious little birds that live on earthworms), frighten a rabbit, and hear numerous squirrels raising a ruckus. When I crossed the small stream dissecting the area, I startled a blue heron and saw a small school of minnows in a leaf cluttered pool. But mostly, I heard me; my crunchy footsteps, my labored breathing, and the rubbing of my jacket against the brush.

After settling in I tried very hard not to move or breathe heavily, in fact I tried to make as little noise as possible. I was in full camouflage gear and blended into the forest floor quite well. Within minutes, the forest came alive. Things I didn't see during my stroll began to appear as if from nowhere. Two raccoons came walking by within a few feet of my position having no idea of my presence. They playfully foraged for food and eventually hopped on a log, walked its length, then disappeared. Their little black masks made them look like bandits from a Scrooge McDuck comic strip.

Squirrels began to move all around me; some on the forest floor and others high in the treetops. Not one or two, but many. They were busy harvesting acorns and storing them away for the winter. I was surprised to see a squirrel pop his head out of a hole in a tree in front of me. He clung to the bark like he had glue on his paws, racing up and down the tree pursuing his passionate activities. To my left I heard a noise, and a button buck moved past stopping to feast on the acorns that were lying all around.

Lest you think this is a scene from Wild Kingdom or Bambi, let me assure you that it really did happen. The critters of the forest came out as soon as they thought I was gone. It's in the stillness that I was able to hear them and witness their activities. It was so awesome I couldn't refrain from saying the word, "Wow!" out loud.

The moment I spoke, it shattered the peaceful setting like the horn of a car screaming in the night. The animals suddenly went on alert, disappearing as if they were water evaporating in the hot sun. As I sat and contemplated the occurrence, I realized that there is nothing in all nature that sounds like the human voice.

Wild animals head for the hills when they hear a human voice, and there is a reason. It is because man is fearfully and wonderfully made in the image of a holy God; our God. You are an amazing being. The animals' reactions are not much different than the New Testament records of men and women reacting to seeing angels: fear, reverence and awe. Today, we are but a shadow of the glorious beings we will be transformed into in heaven, yet we have the imprint of God upon us. The scriptures tell us that we will be rulers, counselors, and we will be exalted by the King!

> *"… man is fearfully and wonderfully made in the image of a holy God; our God. You are an amazing being."*

The next time you're in the woods, take a moment to be still; to be quiet. For it is in the quiet that the truth of who you are, and the reality of your surroundings, are revealed. It is in the quiet that you hear the voice of God and receive the assurance of your salvation. It is in the quiet that you commune with the Resurrected King.

And it is in the quiet that you sense the leading of the Holy Spirit, coming to a greater understanding of the remarkable inheritance that has been given you by your Father. So, go forth in the strength of the Lord you Royal Priest...you Chosen Nation...you Holy People. You are set apart by the Creator.

Psalm 139:1-4 NIV

¹ O LORD, you have searched me and you know me. ² You know when I sit and when I rise; you perceive my thoughts from afar. ³ You discern my going out and my lying down; you are familiar with all my ways. ⁴ Before a word is on my tongue you know it completely, O LORD.

A Bird in my Hands

Walking a Lonely Creek

Six days and thirty-seven years ago, nestled deep in the crook of a tree branch near a meandering stream, an exhausted crow struggled for freedom. His plight was not obvious to a passer-by, yet it was real. The crow was affixed to a length of fishing line high up in a cottonwood tree, common in that area of central Indiana. Dangling on the end of the line was a temptation no bird could resist, least of all a ravenous crow; a bright yellow crappie jig.

Some hapless fisherman, likely still talking about the one that got away, had miscalculated his cast and snagged the lure in the cottonwood. Unable to retrieve it, he pulled on the snag until the string gave way and surrendered the jig high in the tree's recesses. Along came Mr. Crow, delighted to see a tiny yellow morsel inviting him to dinner. He quickly obliged and gulped the fellow down, not knowing that a nasty little hook was about to change his life.

When I happened along, the commotion caught my attention. In the distance, high in a cottonwood tree was a crow. Now that was not so unusual, but this crow was flying. Again, not to uncommon, but this crow was flying in small, perfectly concentric circles, one right after another. Now that was odd. Round and round he would go, stopping occasionally in the crook of the tree branch he was on to rest, then round and round again.

I thought it quite extraordinary until I approached close enough to see a little yellow crappie jig tied on a piece of fishing line. The jig was hooked securely in the crow's beak, and the other end of the line was connected to the tree branch. About four feet separated them. When the crow would take flight trying to win his freedom, he looked like a model airplane tied to a string going around and around its pilot. In this case his earthly bondage was a tree branch holding the bird hostage.

That day I was, as it were, the crow's savior. Slowly I made my way up the branches of the tree until I was thirty feet off the ground. Then I stretched my arm out and leaned over the expanse, barely able to grab the fishing line on the opposite end of the crow. I reeled him in like a fish, but this was a flying fish! Eventually I was able to take the crow in my hands and hold him securely. I had misgivings about being pecked to death; yet as soon as I held him, he understood. He looked at me and stopped all struggling. I removed the jig and threw the crow straight up in the air. He didn't miss a beat and flew higher and higher, eventually disappearing.

Sometimes in life we see something resembling a crappie jig, thinking it's something wonderful. Like the crow, we decide we want it yet are unaware of the dangers linked to our decision. It might be an addiction that forms from substance abuse. It might be a financial decision that puts us in over our heads. Or it might be pride in our life that takes root and churns us like butter. Yet, Jesus is an amazing Savior.

> **"As we fly in circles trying to free ourselves from bad decisions and circumstances, God reins us in, holds us in his gentle hands, and sets us free."**

As we fly in circles trying to free ourselves from bad decisions and circumstances, God reins us in, holds us in his gentle hands, and sets us free. All we have to do is learn a simple lesson from Mr. Crow. We must fix our eyes on our Savior and trust him. He will set us free. Praise God for his Amazing Grace!

2 Corinthians 3:17-18 NIV

[17]Now the Lord is the Spirit, and where the Spirit of the Lord is, there is freedom. [18]And we all, who with unveiled faces contemplate the Lord's glory, are being transformed into his image with ever-increasing glory, which comes from the Lord, who is the Spirit."

Trolling for Hats

Collecting Cranium Cappers

Some people love to collect road hats. For some reason they seem to be the first thing to fly when you stick your head out of a car window. The wind grabs them, gently lifts them to the heavens, then deposits them on an obscure stretch of road to be found by the head-gear treasure hunter. I have a friend with a vast collection of noggin-toppers that he's collected from the streets and byways of this fair land. Though his collection is impressive, I tend to be more discriminating. My past-time of choice is trolling for hats.

Anybody can find a hat by the side of the road, but who can say where a lost hat lies on the bottom of a lake or the pool of a river? Finding them takes stealth, cunning and careful planning. My method of choice is to use a heavy, multi-hooked lure that drags the bottom as I retrieve it, gently twitching my rod when a potential hat has been snagged.

Probably the most irritating thing about trolling for hats is all the fish you catch. Those pesky things, large and small, seem to like the bottom retrieve I use and I'm constantly removing them from my gear. It's a hazard of the activity, yet one not without its benefits. I suppose, if you like the taste of those slippery aquatic vertebrates, you could fill your freezer using this technique; but I prefer the challenge of hat-napping.

I feel a little bit like an archeologist when trolling for hats. I study a body of water, dissect it into grids, then work those grids systematically careful to cover the most likely spots. Beaches, windy points and boat ramps are favorite haunts of those cranium covers.

It takes hours and hours of invested searching to snag one of the little buggers, but the reward is worth it. Sun bonnets, Crocodile Dundee hats, crushables, ball caps; I've seen them all. Like muddy little clams, many have visited the bottom of my bucket, so contorted one can barely discern the creation they were designed to be. Instead of efficient sun-blockers, they look like dirty, soggy clumps of fabric after sitting on the bottom of a lake for a few months. Yet, with a little tender care and cleaning, they become beautiful once again. A little scrubbing, removal of mud and the whitening effects of color-safe bleach, and those shriveled lumps of fabric are restored and useful again for the purpose they were designed and created. A beanie with new purpose, hope and life.

One of the most amazing things about our God is that he not only saves us, but he restores and renews us. We are like dirty, soggy lumps of fabric, dead in our trespasses and sin - lost at the bottom of the darkest waters. Yet our wonderful Savior pulls us out of the sticky mire we are unable to remove ourselves from. He cleans us up,

> **"One of the most amazing things about our God is that he not only saves us, but he restores and renews us."**

stands us up, breathes life into us, and gives us a new path to walk. He takes what is broken and without hope and restores it in holiness and righteousness that we may walk with him without shame or fear. He makes us a new creation and one day, will give us a new body and a new name. There are no words to express the joy and gratitude for this act of mercy.

The next time you look in a mirror, thank God for the person you see. Though still imperfect, you are loved and cherished by the King of Kings. You have value beyond any ability to comprehend. In Christ, you are his child and he will NEVER let you go. Praise be to the Almighty! Oh…and while you're looking in that mirror….try on a few hats!

Romans 8:37-39 NIV

[37] "No, in all these things we are more than conquerors through him who loved us. [38]For I am convinced that neither death nor life, neither angels nor demons, neither the present nor the future, nor any powers, [39]neither height nor depth, nor anything else in all creation, will be able to separate us from the love of God that is in Christ Jesus our Lord."

-Day 4-

The Road Less Traveled

Mountain Meanderings

Robert Frost is a favorite poet of mine, and one of his best-known works is a poem named, "The Road Not Taken."

> Two roads diverged in a yellow wood,
> And sorry I could not travel both
> And be one traveler, long I stood
> And looked down one as far as I could
> To where it bent in the undergrowth;

The poems ends;

> I shall be telling this with a sigh
> Somewhere ages and ages hence;
> Two roads diverged in a wood, and I —
> I took the one less traveled by,
> And that has made all the difference.

Just a few weeks ago, I hiked a trail in Colorado called the Cascade Creek Trail, near Durango. A hike of six miles along a peaceful glen, and through some beautiful woods, revealed several magnificent waterfalls that inspire and heal your soul. God is an amazing and creative artist that has placed on this earth special places that defy description. Some are easily accessed, but most require significant work to observe.

As I exited the truck in the thin mountain air, the smell of balsam filled my nostrils. A gentle breeze drew it from the wooded slopes above me and into the overgrown area I found to park. The creek I was to follow was really a river sending torrents of water down its steep incline, swollen from the melting snow.

The morning was sunny, and the aspen were true to their Latin name, *Populus tremuloides*. As if trembling from the cold, their newly emerged leaves shimmered in the sunlight, dark on one side and light on the other. They bent the light and rattled on their branches as the breeze playfully bounced them around. Standing like sentinels above them, the Douglas fir rose high into the sky enveloping the warmth of the morning sun.

I threw my pack on, filled with water for the long hike. The weight was more than I was used to, and the 10,000-foot elevation soon proved to be a challenge. Sounding like a steam locomotive climbing a grade, I drew in air laboring for the little oxygen it held, often stopping just to breathe. Had the trail been flat perhaps the work would have been less, but this trail, carved into the rock and hillsides, gained a total of 1,500 feet over its course to the falls. If I had joined the crew of a fishing vessel, they would have called me a landlubber. On a ship, it often takes weeks to acclimate to the rolling seas, and so it is with altitude. It can take weeks to acclimate to the thinner air. I was alone with our little dog, and of course God.

I chose to take the road less traveled, why? It was filled with hardship, hard work, exhaustion, and even fear. Two days before a bear was harassing a family near there. I diligently included a can of bear-spray (a cayenne pepper-based spray that is said to deter the bruins), but an encounter would have taken my already racing heart to a grand crescendo. Like the tympani in the 1812 overture, it would have thundered throughout the woods.

Why did I go to all this work? Because of the prize. The waterfalls are some of the most beautiful in Colorado. Though the work was hard, there was beauty and joy along the way, and oh the prize! It's worth every effort you can muster.

Isn't our Christian life like that? We are called to take the road less traveled and to endure some hardship. At times it's not easy, yet the road is placed there for us to travel, benefiting us. And on it we experience the joy of knowing the Lord Jesus Christ.

"As you walk the road less traveled, find joy in your journey, and peace in your heart, and fix your eyes on the Pioneer and Perfecter of your faith."

It is Jesus Christ who died on a cross to pay the price of our sin that we may have eternal life. That is unimaginable! Yet He did it for the joy set before Him: you, and me.

As you walk the road less traveled, find joy in your journey, and peace in your heart, and fix your eyes on the Pioneer and Perfecter of your faith. He is faithful to see you down that road and to usher you into His presence. And oh, the prize! To gaze on the face of your Savior and to enjoy Him forever. Amen!

Hebrews 12:1-2 NIV

[1]*"Therefore, since we are surrounded by such a great cloud of witnesses, let us throw off everything that hinders and the sin that so easily entangles. And let us run with perseverance the race marked out for us, [2]fixing our eyes on Jesus, the pioneer and perfecter of faith. For the joy set before him he endured the cross, scorning its shame, and sat down at the right hand of the throne of God."*

There is a Season
A Perfect Image

It wasn't that long ago that my hair was its natural color, a darker shade looking a little like chocolate ice cream that's melted in a bowl; a creamy light brown. But now when I look in a mirror, I see white. First it was speckles, then streaks, and now a full-blown invasion of little white soldiers all lined up in formation and doing the bidding of my comb. Each one has enlisted for life (I hope).

Suddenly my life has become a sober reminder of my father. When I look in a mirror it seems he's staring at me though the voice coming from his mouth is mine. Scary! My brother, though a handsome man, has a small circle of skin beginning to show through his hair on the back of his head. White hair is one thing, but the possibility of losing my hair could throw me into a premature state of grieving. It's difficult to lose a friend or a loved one, but to lose hundreds of them on a regular basis over an extended period of time is more than I can cope with.

Each of us goes through a natural, God ordained, process of aging that defines our periods of life. The scriptures even state that white hair is a crown. While I agree, my crown seems to have been delivered a little early. I think the Crown-Giver has confused me with an older gentleman. Why it was just yesterday that I was pulling Michelle's pigtails in third grade.

And not long ago that mom was packing my lunch box and sending me off to school.

OK, I confess, that was a little longer ago than yesterday, but it was very recently that I met my wife Becky and fell in love forever…well…that was a few years ago too, I guess. But I remember like it was this morning holding our first little daughter, Ellen, snug to my chest and kissing her little forehead. She was a miracle. She's turning how old? Forty?!

I guess I really am as old as I look. I have seen a lot of water pass under the little bridge I sit on. And I am the man God created and has walked with for 63 years, sustaining me through impossible circumstances and desperate appeals. I am the man that God laughed with during the birth of our children and even now is preparing a place for in heaven. And I am also the man who God, in his divine wisdom, has chosen to add some white hair to. Besides, I'm getting closer to the time when remembering what my hair looks like will be a struggle because I may not remember where the refrigerator is (though I doubt it), or where my house is, or even what my name is.

There is little, if anything we can control. The sun will rise and set, the rain will fall, and the morning

"…our future is not ours to control, our present is not ours to wield, rather all things come from God the Father."

dew will be harvested by thousands of creatures. Life will begin and end, the wind will blow where it wills, and the caterpillar will build a cocoon only to be transformed into a beautiful creature. You see, our future is not ours to control, our present is not ours to wield, rather all things come from God the Father.

Only one thing is required of us; to love God and then to enjoy him forever. Not a difficult job description. No performance quotas and no labor. He has provided for his children the greatest gift ever to be given; **himself**. He is the very essence of selflessness. He is the expression of surrender. He is the Salvation for all generations.

As you bustle around in the busyness of your day, remember that God has ordered those days. He has created you perfectly. You are a perfect image of the Father. You are a royal priest and you belong to His holy nation. You are royalty; a prince in the royal family with full access to the King. And He loves you without reserve. His plans are perfect - your life is His. Pick up your "prayer-phone" and dial up God. He is ready to listen, to heal and to transform you. He will dress you in royal splendor for all eternity.

Psalm 136 :1-3 NIV

¹ Give thanks to the Lord, for he is good. His love endures forever. ² Give thanks to the God of gods. His love endures forever. ³ Give thanks to the Lord of lords: His love endures forever.

-Day 6-

A Normal Morning
Tenacity Exemplified

The sun felt warm as rays laden with heat met me, first hitting my feet and finally my face as the garage door opened. The creak of the door reminded me that I needed to buy a can of oil to spray on the partially rusted rollers. I noticed a new blemish on the driver's door of my car and remembered parking at the local hardware store last night while I ran in for some weed killer. "Likely a rogue shopping cart, or maybe a careless patron," I thought. It seems nearly impossible to keep anything in pristine condition in today's society. As I unlocked the doors to get into my car, the driver's door lock stuck and wouldn't open. It's a problem the car has had for a few years but was never a great enough nuisance to repair. I used the key to turn the lock and it gave way begrudgingly. "I really need to fix that. I'm going to get stuck one day."

I started the car and slowly backed it out of the narrow opening and into the drive. The morning was pleasant and inviting. My route to work was the same every day. Turn right out of the drive, another right at the stop sign and a left at the next. The route puts me on a country road leading to town. Expansive fields planted in corn edge both sides of the road and a local "round-a-bout" slows all traffic to an acceptable speed.

As I entered the round-a-bout, I glance into my driver's side mirror and noticed a small brown spider that had constructed a make-shift web covering part of the reflective surface during the night. He sat right in the middle of the web waiting for a tasty morsel to become entwined in his sticky trap. He was so small that my view was not impaired, but I was certainly distracted.

As I accelerated, the wind caught the web and it began bouncing back and forth, slamming the little spider against the mirror. At first, he tried to attach more anchor points, but eventually the web shook so violently that he curled up in a little ball to wait it out. Shortly after the round-a-bout, I came to a stop light and settled behind a line of cars waiting for the green. Instantly the little spider went to work, sensing a shift in his favor.

He ran to the edge at the bottom of the mirror and laid several more strings of webbing. He then attached these to the main structure that had just taken the beating to strengthen it. All this he accomplished in less than 30 seconds. Then, to my amazement, he centered himself in the web again. Now any rational spider would have realized that he was hitch hiking on a fuming beast and should hide until it was parked under a shady tree. At that point, though completely separated from family, he could make a new life in one of the trees...but no...not my spider. He was going to get a meal come wind or rain!

As I accelerated through the light and landed at a cruising speed of 55mph, the little web began to shake violently again. Over and over the little spider slammed into the mirror like a fastball at Yankee Stadium, and the battered arachnid rolled into a ball once again. It was an epic struggle; spider against wind. He realized his plight and shot strings of web from his little balled body. They stuck all over the mirror. I felt bad for the little spider having grown to appreciate his work ethic and having witnessed his interminable will. Yet I was in a line of traffic and had no ability to pull over and save him.

Eventually the laws of physics prevailed. The force of the wind tore the entire web loose except for the main tether that connected the spider's abdomen to the mirror. For a moment it looked like he was bungee jumping horizontally. He bounced back and forth at the end of the tether until it finally broke. His little brown body shot past my window like a missile, eventually disappearing in the rearview. I felt like I'd lost a dear friend. He didn't do anything wrong. He was scrawny and needed some food, and maybe a little unaware.

Remember the old adage, "What you don't know won't hurt you?" We'll, it's not true. As Christians we are told to be wise, be discerning, and to train our minds making them sharp like a sword. We're also told to test every spirit, and with good reason.

What we don't know *can* hurt us. It is why God has laid his Holy Word out for us through the Bible. His Word is the way things should be. As Christians, we too easily

> **"What we don't know can hurt us. It is why God has laid his Holy Word out for us through the Bible."**

become complacent and even dulled by the world we live in. Like the spider, there are dangers that we cannot see, yet God's faithfulness and the instruction he provides will see us safely through this life and escort us with joy into His presence. Don't build your web on the mirror of a fuming beast, and don't lay the foundation of your home in the sand. Rather, stand firm on the Rock of Christ; our Hope and Redeemer.

1 Peter 5:6-11 NIV

[6]*"Humble yourselves, therefore, under God's mighty hand, that he may lift you up in due time.* [7] *Cast all your anxiety on him because he cares for you.* [8] *Be alert and of sober mind. Your enemy the devil prowls around like a roaring lion looking for someone to devour.* [9] *Resist him, standing firm in the faith, because you know that the family of believers throughout the world is undergoing the same kind of sufferings.* [10] *And the God of all grace, who called you to his eternal glory in Christ, after you have suffered a little while, will himself restore you and make you strong, firm and steadfast.* [11] *To him be the power for ever and ever. Amen."*

Snake!

Cobra Caper

Each of us is a walking story. We are a compilation of decisions and choices made throughout our lives which result in who we are today. The paths we have walked, the decisions we have made, and the focus of our lives make up our story. Within those stories is the sovereign will of God, showing up at times we didn't expect, only to find he's been there all along.

Shortly after our second child was born my wife and I moved to a backwoods area in southern Indiana. We purchased a rundown historic log cabin built in the mid 1800's that was constructed with hand hewn square logs. The cabin sat back in the woods and had a steep driveway meandering up the hill where it sat.

In the spring of that year a friend called me for some help. He wanted me to build a number of cages at his business; a serpentarium. For those wondering, a serpentarium is like the snake exhibit at the zoo. It was a building filled with every type of snake and reptile you can imagine.

I went to work building the cages, yet an uneasy feeling settled over me. Day after day I would walk past scaly serpents from all around the world, each sticking their vile little tongues out at me. My friend Beau walked in one morning holding a plastic bag filled with white (expired) rats; the food of choice for many of his snakes. He nonchalantly asked me if I would like to observe him feeding one of his snakes. I thought, what harm could there be in that? It actually sounded pretty interesting. I was clueless.

We stepped into the next room. There in front of me was a glass cage with two 14-foot-long King Cobras; the snakes he was about to feed. Remember that our lives are made up of decisions, some good, some bad. What is amazing is that God always shows up and loves to rescue us, even when we make bad decisions – he loves us that much.

Have you ever experienced your mind saying, "run-fast" but your feet wouldn't move? That is where I found myself. I reasoned, "My friend has been around snakes all his life. There shouldn't be any problems. Besides, the snakes look pretty docile."

Beau slid the glass door open about a foot and using a tool called a "snake hook" pinned the head of one of the cobras to the bottom of the cage. He grasped the neck right behind the head and lifted it to begin shoving a rat down its throat. As I mentioned, the snake was no small critter, but again I reasoned, "My friend is a buff and powerful man, there shouldn't be any problem. At least the snake was moving now - very interesting."

I don't know if you've ever had someone pin *your* head to the floor by grabbing your neck and forcefully shoving you down, but I don't think you'd like it, and so the cobra did not like it. In a flash the snake reared up taking Beau's hand with him. All 14 feet of the serpent shot out of the cage while he hung on for dear life. I jumped back and watched an epic battle; man against beast. Beau had both hands around the now swollen neck of the snake, staring him in the eyes. He was writhing back and forth trying to control it and losing ground fast. Out of the frenzy of activity I heard Beau yell, "Grab its tail!"

I wanted to respond, "You talkin' to me?" but I realized that Beau was in a life or death struggle. If the snake won, Beau was toast and I was next on the menu! The cobra had "hooded" (a little trick that tells everyone around that he's not a happy camper). The hood was so large that Beau was unable to lock his fingers together to secure it. And then the decision; I grabbed the tail of that 14-foot pulsating monster and hung on with purpose.

I'm sure that most of you have not grabbed the tail of a 14-foot King Cobra. Let me assure you; they are very strong. In addition, they are cold, scaly and clammy. I felt, however, that I had no choice. I actually liked Beau and would rather face the cobra than his wife should I have to tell her of his demise. To review: Beau had both hands around the hood of the snake, it was bearing its fangs in Beau's face, Beau was being thrown all around the room by the powerful snake, and now I was being tossed left and right, hanging onto its massive tail. It was like a bad ride at the carnival.

Then I heard four words I never want to hear again; Beau said, "I can't hold on!" - not good…in fact, not good at all. Decision time again. Should I release the snake and run, or hang on? The decision was made for me. Beau suddenly lost his grip and the snake went for me. I dropped its tail and began running to the corner of the room, backwards. Before I had taken two steps, the snake shot right between my legs and headed for the same corner. I reeled around, and there, 10 feet from me, the snake was raised up, fully hooded and vehemently hissing. The snake had risen so high that I was looking up at it. Beau grabbed a special snake handling pole with a rope on the end and carefully worked the noose around the snake's neck, managing to control it.

Decisions, life changing decisions, they tell the stories of our lives. It was clear that God saved us from the serpent, and I had no interest in a repeat performance! Beau found someone else to build the cages.

If you haven't read the books of Kings, I would encourage you to do so. They are a compilation of stories; stories of leaders and how they directed their lives through daily decisions. Though our outward decisions affect others, it is our heart that God looks at. Probably the most difficult part of reading

"The book of Kings is a stark reminder that each of us has that choice. How we choose to answer the call of God in our life will determine the end of our story."

the books of Kings is that every story ends in one of two ways: either it says that the king followed God all the days of his life and was laid to rest with his fathers, or it says that the king did evil in the sight of the Lord. The book of Kings is a stark reminder that each of us has that choice. How we choose to answer the call of God in our life will determine the end of our story.

May you dwell with the Most High in your heart. May you live a life directed by the Holy One. I can't wait to read your story! A day will come when all of God's people will hear of the faithfulness of His Church; His people.

Psalm 139:23-24 NIV

> [23] *Search me, O God, and know my heart;*
>   *test me and know my anxious thoughts.*

> [24] *See if there is any offensive way in me,*
>   *and lead me in the way everlasting.*

-Day 8-

<h1 style="text-align:center;">Walking with My Savior</h1>

Peace on the Mountain

Over the summer months last year, I had the opportunity to visit some amazing places in Colorado. In July I visited one of the most beautiful small mountain lakes I have ever seen. Monarch Lake is nestled in the mountains at 8,400 feet just south of Rocky Mountain National Park. It sits at the end of a 9-mile-long dirt road that turns to a gooey mess after a rain. Right before the trailhead for the lake, a wild rushing river drops steeply through the aspen, sub-alpine and Douglas-fir forest that populates the slopes.

As I parked the truck and opened the door a strong blast of balsam filled my nostrils tickling the olfactory receptors located along that path. The scent hit my brain, poignantly reminding me of pleasant memories of hikes through similar forests. It is one of my favorite smells and never fails to put me in the most congenial of moods.

Pulling on my backpack and locking the truck, I headed out for a morning of fishing and hiking. The air was cool, and the piney squirrels were abuzz on the forest floor. Only small patches of snow remained from the long winter and they were already busy preparing for the next. As I summited a small hill, the lake lay before me, water so blue it's hard to imagine. Small islands with fir trees clutching their barren rocks dotted the lake, only adding to its grandeur. Jagged peaks still capped with snow framed the lake behind and on both sides.

The trail around the lake wound up and down the terrain, taking nearly 5 miles to complete its route. It meandered through some very dense wilderness that extended for many miles. It was part of the 395 square miles of National Forest abutting the celebrated mountains of one of our most loved National Parks.

As I began hiking around the lake, I spotted three moose crossing the river that exited the body of water. They worked their way across a slack in the rapids and disappeared into the woods. I continued up the trail and remember feeling particularly close to God. As I hiked, I talked with him and thanked him for the amazing place he had created. And he spoke back. He comforted me, encouraged me and lifted my head high. My heart swelled to bursting.

After several miles, near a high clearing, I saw bright rays of sun shining on an area filled with aspen. I diverted from the trail and headed for the aspen. When I reached them and stepped into the trees, I was overwhelmed with the splendor before me. The light reflecting on the white bark of the trees lit up the area and the breeze made their leaves dance in the sunlight. The smell of the aspen was incredible; and my soul, once again, was stirred. I had to stop and talk to God.

My soul groaned, even ached to be in the presence of God. I could hear the certainty of His words as they permeated my heart, "Son, you *are* in my presence. I dwell within you. We will never be separated." That truth settled deep within me and confirmed in my spirit that we in fact, would be together forever. He promises it in his scripture, and he is the Promise Keeper.

> **"My soul groaned, even ached to be in the presence of God."**

I can imagine a similar scene in Genesis when God walked and communed with Adam. Walking in the garden, surrounded by immense beauty and talking to the one he loved passionately. All that, and more, will be restored. That perfect fellowship will once again take place, for God loves you beyond measure and will work everything out according to his perfect will. May you experience a deep and intimate walk with your Savior as you seek to live a life that honors the King.

2 Corinthians 5:1-3 NIV

[1]Now we know that if the earthly tent we live in is destroyed, we have a building from God, an eternal house in heaven, not built by human hands. [2]Meanwhile we groan, longing to be clothed with our heavenly dwelling, [3]because when we are clothed, we will not be found naked.

Lord, our Lord, how majestic is your name in all the earth! Psalm 8:9 NIV

Act Your Age

Crash Landing

The pain was beyond anything I had ever experienced, except for the surgery I had shortly after getting married. My pulsating synapses' shot messages of objection through every muscle fiber in my body quickly focusing on a small area in my lower back. I lay spread out in the snow on a steep slope looking as if I was ready to make a snow angel...the last thing on my mind. As my eyes came back into focus, I could see big fluffy white clouds contrasted against a blue sky. For a brief moment I thought, "Everything will be fine. The pain will only last a moment." Optimism, though helpful mentally, simply distanced me further from the truth.

The sledding hill I attacked that winter afternoon was part of an 18-hole golf course that offered families the opportunity to slide down its steep terrain. Great fun was had by all, that is unless you were an out-of-shape middle-aged gentleman that still thought he could keep up with the kiddos. I should have taken a clue from my initial observations of screaming young children who disappeared down the hill at lighting speeds. They would disappear over a hill and then suddenly reappear for a brief moment, only to disappear again.

"That's odd," I thought scoping the hill from the top. "As steep as this hill is, I don't understand how the kids would reappear after completely disappearing...strange." What I quickly found was that there was a sharp bump in the snow about two thirds of the way down. As the sledders hit it, they flew about five feet in the air, making them visible from the top again, but only for a brief moment. As I approached the bump at break-neck speed on my plastic saucer, the scene was surreal. Bodies were flying into the air as if from a trampoline, doing all types of flips and gymnastics; most landing far from their sled in a heap.

The answer to my question was clarified too late, for it came only after I was within feet of the menacing bump at a speed rivaling the space shuttle's re-entry into Earth's atmosphere. I would guess most of you have been in a situation that required some pretty quick thinking followed by some aggressive and risky action to save you from certain disaster, correct? Perhaps it was a quick maneuver to avoid hitting something with your car, or a careful exit to avoid a difficult conversation. Well suffice it to say that my ole' body didn't have enough moves left in it to miss the bump. In fact, it would have been challenging for a cat to pull off.

I only had moments to firmly grasp the saucer I was sitting in and hang on for dear life; then I felt the impact and the lift. Up I went, sled in hand, flying through the air over the snow. Wind whistled past my head, tugging at my ear lobes sticking out from under my stocking cap. I thought, "I must look like an alien in his flying saucer, skimming over the snow." And for a moment it was fun. I felt free like a bird soaring through the sky.

The worst part of jumping from a cliff is the landing. For those who do so with parachutes on their backs, the experience is exhilarating. They have an opportunity to feel the wind against their faces and to experience a form of weightlessness, at least a mental manifestation of it. Well, I can attest to the fact that the worse part of flying into the air at supersonic speeds on a sled is also the landing. No landing gear, no parachute, no safe bubble, just body and bone impacting the hard-packed snow. And that is how I came to be lying on a steep slope, on my back, in the snow.

After about 3 minutes, I attempted to move...nothing worked. I could wiggle my fingers, but I was pretty much numb from the neck down. I was able to cock my head enough to see that another exuberant sledder was about to scalp me with the runners on his joy machine. With purposeful effort, I managed to roll perpendicular to the hill one or two times, just enough to avoid the collision. The pain was excruciating. Searing stabs of discomfort attacked my lower back like a pit-bull attacking some nefarious biped.

After this tremendous effort, I found myself in the same circumstance as before; lying on my back on the hill with multiple targets approaching at light-speed. Garnering all of the focus I could muster, I managed to get into a crawling position and slowly work my way off of the hill into a section of trees where I'd be safe. My back sounded like a car with broken springs. Every move I made was accompanied by cracks, squeaks and groans as my skeletal system tried to realign with my muscles.

With relief I fell behind a tree where I was safe. As I fell behind the tree, I found that the snow there was quite deep. My plastic disk was AWOL, likely still flying like a Frisbee to the creek below, so I had no way to support myself. Down I went into four feet of snow, on my back and hidden from view to anyone who may come by. Miraculously, since I was on my back again, I was able to breathe. So, there I was, nearly buried in the snow, in the woods, on a steep slope with only my boots sticking into the air to reveal my presence. Good grief! I felt like the bad guys in Home Alone 2 trying to move around after being pummeled by bricks and shocked by an electric welder, except my hair didn't "poof!"

I'm sure I'm not the only one who has ever had a battle with pride, but I then did the unthinkable. Moments later a young man walked by and said, "Hey man are you okay? I saw you take quite a spill." Any normal individual would have said, "No, I'm not OK. I rolled down here after a terrible car accident that threw me from my vehicle. I've been here for days and I think my pelvis is broken. Call mountain rescue!" But I didn't. I was embarrassed and said, "Yes, I'm fine. Did you like the choreographed moves I did? I've been practicing them for months."

The Good Samaritan looked at me puzzled and walked off and there I was again: broken, alone and buried in the snow. After about 10 minutes of being MIA, one of the men from our church who was sledding with our family came to look for me. He'd received a tip from some guy named G. Samaritan that a crazy man was burrowed up under a tree halfway down the hill, and he assumed it was me. By the time he found me some feeling was coming back into my arms and legs. "Are you alright man?" he asked in earnest.

"Oh, I'm fine," I said, "just taking a little rest under this tree. Could you help me up? I'm feeling a little tired."

Scratching his head, he started pulling on my arms to extricate me from the hole I was in. As he did, I began to sing loudly and in earnest. I can't remember the song, but it had several colorful metaphors in it that relayed the pain and displeasure I was experiencing. A ballad, I think. I ended the song with a finale similar to the final bars of the 1812 overture. It sounded like cannon fire and black powder exploding as he finally dragged me to my feet. Sweat was pouring down my face and freezing into little icicles around my mustache. "You sure you're OK?" he asked again. You were slightly off pitch on those last 5 notes. Not like you at all."

"Yes, I'm fine, just warming up for choir practice this evening," I replied. I felt like a Buick Skylark had just run over me! Slowly, with great effort from my friend and from me, one foot in front of the other, I worked my way up the hill until finally I was sitting on a bench overlooking the golf course. I didn't move from that spot for nearly an hour. "Daddy aren't you going to sled anymore?" one of my children asked. "No honey," I replied, "I want to sit here and soak in the beauty of the day!"

Many Christians live in denial. We deny that problems in our lives are serious. We think we can control a particular situation, or we refuse to see how even a little problem impacts those around us. We go on living

"Many Christians live in denial. We deny that problems in our lives are serious."

in bondage because we're unwilling to acknowledge and deal with those areas of our lives that are consuming us. And yet Jesus has already provided for our freedom, including freedom from the bondage of sin.

As I crawled off of the sledding hill, I could have laughed at myself, I could have raised the alarm and sought help, or I could have cried out to God, but I didn't do any of those things. Instead, I was so worried about how I might appear to others that I was a fake, a disingenuous counterfeit, even when I was only confronting myself. I laid there broken and in pain, yet I wanted to appear "together" to those around me.

And we often do the same thing with God. We act as if we have it all together; as if we're perfect saints. But God sees our hearts. We can hide nothing from him. He doesn't expect us to be perfect, but he does expect us to be real; to be brutally honest about who we are, especially with Him. I had a dear friend tell me once, "Talk to God, yell at Him if you must, but share your heart with him." He is faithful to listen and meet you right where you are.

Roman 8:18-23 NIV

[18]I consider that our present sufferings are not worth comparing with the glory that will be revealed in us. [19]The creation waits in eager expectation for the sons of God to be revealed. [20]For the creation was subjected to frustration, not by its own choice, but by the will of the one who subjected it, in hope [21]that the creation itself will be liberated from its bondage to decay and brought into the glorious freedom of the children of God.

-Day 10-

Failure
Claws of Pain

The dog came running down the street toward the open garage door where my daughter Lianna and I stood. We were enjoying the fresh air of spring as we picked up some of the mess accumulated in the garage bays over the long winter in Park City, Utah. The interloper spied our family pet, Missy, and made a beeline for her.

Missy was a find, a lean black cat found in desperate need during one of our trips to the local mall. She lay quivering under a stairway soaking wet from the spring rain. She was skittish, untrusting and nervous about our attention that day. Yet, she compliantly gave way to our encouragement, and eventual tugs, as we tried to coax her from the hiding place where she rested.

"Poor little kitty," Lianna ejected through shivering lips and chattering teeth. Cold, wet, miserable little Missy was scooped into her arms for a free ride to the Dare Rescue Center, Inc. We had been in business for many years, finding every possible stray in a tri-state area and providing for their needs. Dogs, cats, frogs and many others found refuge, warmth and friendship in our humble home.

Missy had grown to love our family, fiercely independent yet always ready to give a little leg rub to the ones she loved, leaving patches of fine black hair on the beneficiaries of her affection. She would gush with approval one minute and the next would smite you with a single look of distain. It really was an emotional roller coaster, never truly knowing where you stood with Missy, queen of the realm. Yet we loved her.

When the lab-sized mutt sauntered into our garage, I encouraged Lianna to quickly pick up Missy lest our little friend be swallowed in one gulp by the irreverent beast. Before the words had finished exiting my mouth, I realized I had made a mistake. It was like a slow-motion scene during an action movie. I could see everything happening yet had no ability to stop it.

She bent down and picked up Missy who had already spied the dog weighing some 70 pounds more than her. Missy had immediately sprung into self-defense mode drawing on all weapons in her arsenal. She bared her teeth, her back was arched, her hissing was like a siren, and her claws appeared ready to do battle. Then, her natural instinct to run kicked in. All four legs began flailing as if her life depended on it. The only problem was that she was still attached to Lianna's hands. Long, painful wounds appeared on the bare skin of her forearms inflicted by the gyrations of a wildcat praying in earnest for a little traction.

Lianna shifted her grasp and the little demon was able to dig deep into the side of her neck with her back legs, satisfying her need for momentum. In a flash Missy powered out of her hands and sprinted away, all the while sending up a chorus of enigmatic iterations that would make a feline blush. No love...no affection...just raw deliberate actions that to this day have left their mark with resolve. The dog did a one eighty, nearly flipping upside down and bulleted off, all the while barking and saying something like, "I see the kitty...I want the kitty...but what a scary kitty!" or something like that.

There stood Lianna, a bloody representation of the girl she used to be, crying and looking at me with anger in her little green eyes. I could see and feel the look. "Daddy, you told me to pick up Missy. You didn't tell me that I would give two pints of blood through multiple lacerations. I trusted you Daddy!" It looked like my little girl had been mowed over by a weed-eater. Few people cross paths with a wildcat and leave unscathed.

All I could think of while I wiped the blood from Lianna's wounds was how I had let my little girl down. No excuses, no rewinding the clock, just unadulterated failure and unpolished malfunction. I felt sick, not knowing what to do, not knowing what to say. Then my little cherub gave me a gift, a gift I didn't deserve. She released me in a moment from my chains of guilt. She looked at me with her big eyes and said, "It's OK daddy. I forgive you. Missy was just scared."

Have you ever come to a place in your life where you've experienced complete failure and no matter how badly you wanted to fix the problem, you couldn't? It's a humbling place

"Have you ever come to a place in your life where you've experienced complete failure and no matter how badly you wanted to fix the problem, you couldn't?"

to be. The world would tell you that in such a place there is no hope, yet God tells us through his Word that there is a Savior, a Lifter of Heads, a Restorer...One who is the very essence of hope.

Has Jesus held your face in his hands and said, "I forgive you"? Has he washed you with his blood and cleansed you from all unrighteousness? You see, sin is no joke, and He is no joke. Sin eats away at the very fabric of who you are. There is no polish, there are no words, there is no action that will wash away that sin apart from the blood of the Sacrificial Lamb, the Merciful Father, the Prince of Peace.

Oh, what a Savior we have! He washes you with hyssop making you whiter than snow. He loves you beyond measure and heals your wounds. He transforms you from the inside out for His glory and honor. He has grafted you into His holy family, the Church of Christ. What a family we have! What a Father we serve!

Isaiah 40:28-31 NIV

28Do you not know? Have you not heard? The Lord is the everlasting God, the Creator of the ends of the earth. He will not grow tired or weary, and his understanding no one can fathom. 29 He gives strength to the weary and increases the power of the weak.30 Even youths grow tired and weary, and young men stumble and fall; 31 but those who hope in the Lord will renew their strength. They will soar on wings like eagles; they will run and not grow weary; they will walk and not be faint.

-Day 11-

The Power of Prayer

Divine Intervention

I worked my way up a steep wooded slope deep in Yellowwood Forest in southern Indiana. My heart was racing, both from the exertion and anxiety of the situation. The ground was slippery from a recent rain and brambles clutched my jeans like scaly little hands reaching from the forest floor. The dew hanging on a spiderweb, meticulously created by some industrious arachnid, splatted onto my face as I pushed through it in the chilled morning air. "Oh crud," I thought as I wiped the sticky boobytrap from my cheek.

Behind me was a half mile of underbrush and muddy footprints made hastily through the dense trees, and before me was the unknown; no understanding of terrain and no concept of distance. I was earnestly seeking a friend. A friend who had called my wife an hour before and said, "I am ending it all. I have taken a bottle of sleeping pills and I'm heading into the woods to die and be with Jesus." I was on a steep slope behind her squatter's shanty-cabin looking for her. No one else knew of the situation and I knew she didn't have much time.

"Where are you?" I asked out loud. The sound of my voice broke the stillness of the woods echoing in the surrounding trees. I began to get my breath under control as streams of vapor bellowed from my nostrils. I summited the incline and stepped into a sizable clearing. A haze of moisture hung on the meadow, twisting the sunlight back and forth creating shimmering points of light that seemed to dance across the top of the grass. The beauty caught me off guard. I thought, "This is a holy place. God is here."

I quickly ran around the circumference of the meadow looking for any sign of our friend. I found five animal trails exiting the meadow at different locations. But which one should I follow? Calling her name several times, I realized I really had no idea if she had come this way yet believed I was looking in the right area. Then it came to me. I was standing in what I'd just judged to be a holy place. Why not ask God where she is?

I stepped to the very center of the clearing and knelt in the wet grass. Bowing my head and folding my hands I asked God, "Where is she Lord? Which trail should I take?" A ray of sunlight broke through the clouds and landed on me warming my back and head. As if some unseen force was directing me, I stood up, turned to my right, and saw the head of one of the trails. I began to follow it. Not a hundred feet from the meadow, there was our friend laying in the trail, unconscious. Then I realized that the unseen force was the hand of God having mercy on one of His children.

She was breathing but in a comatose state. I picked her up, threw her over my shoulder, and ran over a mile to the nearest house. I was able to break into the house and use their phone to call an ambulance. After several days in the hospital, she stabilized and is alive today. In fact, we just spoke with her a few months ago.

As Christians, we tend to live believing that God exists and that He loves us, yet we are unfamiliar with the deep relationship God wants to have with us. We believe in Him yet are surprised when He miraculously intervenes in our lives. Let me encourage you. God is more real than the world you live in and see around you. He is the very thing that holds us together and is the source of life.

As Christians, we are well versed in the events that took place in the Bible throughout history, yet we struggle to trust and experience God in our own lives. We quickly tout the love and power of God as related throughout history yet struggle to testify of His power in us. Seeing things properly requires a paradigm shift. We must go from being historians to becoming eyewitnesses, testifying of what God is doing in *our* lives, *now*. As you fix your eyes on Christ, know that He loves you and is interceding, *right now*, on your behalf. That takes your prayers from hopeful, to confidence-filled and powerful!

> **"We must go from being historians to becoming eyewitnesses, testifying of what God is doing in *our* lives, *now*."**

2 Peter 1:16-18 NIV

16 For we did not follow cleverly devised stories when we told you about the coming of our Lord Jesus Christ in power, but we were eyewitnesses of his majesty. 17 He received honor and glory from God the Father when the voice came to him from the Majestic Glory, saying, "This is my Son, whom I love; with him I am well pleased." 18 We ourselves heard this voice that came from heaven when we were with him on the sacred mountain.

Jude 1:24-25 NIV   Blessing

24To him who is able to keep you from falling and to present you before his glorious presence without fault and with great joy— 25to the only God our Savior be glory, majesty, power and authority, through Jesus Christ our Lord, before all ages, now and forevermore! Amen.

-Day 12-

Fear

Walking on the Edge

"It's OK. Don't look down!" The command echoed off of the walls of the steep cliffs falling away below us.

"I can't do it, Daddy," my 10-year-old daughter communicated, tears rolling down her cheeks. "I just can't do it."

The day had started like any other vacation. We all slept in that morning enjoying our warm hotel beds only 30 miles from the north rim of the Grand Canyon. After a great time of devotions, the girls got up and prepared for a day of sightseeing and fun. On the agenda was a mule ride down the rim trail, lunch at the lodge restaurant, a short hike along the top, and a commitment to watch the sunset over the huge expanse.

The Grand Canyon is just that, grand! It is one of the most amazing works God has placed on the earth. The subtle hues of reds and browns melting together in the vastness are something only He could envision and accomplish. It's as if God sat down with an empty canvas and a set of watercolors to paint a picture as no one else could, yet it's not a picture, rather a living, breathing part of creation.

That evening, as we searched for a spot to watch the "world-class" sunset over the canyon, we noticed a number of people walking out onto a point jutting into seemingly thin air. The rock was quite wide as it began its journey away from the rim. After twenty feet it narrowed to five feet wide for a short expanse and then ended in a thirty-foot diameter plateau. Out we scurried, eyes on our goal; the perfect spot to watch a sunset!

It wasn't until we were actually standing on the final section of rock that we looked down. There below us the sheer rock wall dropped a thousand feet. Suddenly, we felt as though we were standing on the tip of the Space Needle in Seattle. Everyone was a little "woozy" from the height, but we stood near the center of the plateau and enjoyed a great sunset.

As we prepared to leave, we were faced with a new obstacle; the five-foot-wide section that we had crossed before. This time however, we were crossing it with new knowledge. That knowledge consisted of the understanding that a misstep would spell certain death. I sauntered across it to show my children that all was well and behind me came all of my darlings, except one, Nadine. She took one look at the task at hand, carefully weighed the risks and said, "No!"

Light was quickly slipping away so I tested her resolve. "Now honey, it's OK. You've done harder things than this. Just look at where you're going and walk quickly across." She took one step onto the rock corridor and began shaking like a surfer in a snowstorm: uncontrollably. She quickly stepped back and began to cry.

"It's OK. Don't look down!"

"I can't do it Daddy; I just can't do it."

I began to contemplate the cost of a helicopter rescue in the Grand Canyon. The cost to fly one from an airport is ridiculous and I couldn't image what a canyon rescue would set me back. I started to walk back out on the narrow section to help when I too was struck with the panic bug. Suddenly, coaxing her seemed like a better idea than rescuing her. After all, what would my children and wife do without a father and husband? I loosened my collar and took some deep breathes. It seemed to help.

"OK Nadine," I said with all the courage I could muster, "Here's what I want you to do. I know you can do this."

"OK Daddy," she said through the tears.

"I want you to get on your hands and knees, close to the rock. Good. Now I want you to look up and fix your eyes on mine. Don't look up or down, or sideways, but fix your eyes on my eyes. I will direct you. Make one small movement at a time until I am holding you in my arms. Okay?" I asked. "Just look in your father's eyes."

She agreed. Slowly, painstakingly, she began to work her way across the narrow section. Somehow looking

"She focused intently never looking up or down, or right or left, gazing into my eyes all the way across until she was snug in my arms."

into her daddy's purposeful eyes provided enough assurance that she was able to muster a bit of courage. She trusted her life to me. She focused intently, never looking up or down, or right or left, gazing into my eyes all the way across until she was snug in my arms. We all were relieved and had a family hug as she stepped into safety. What a joy to hold that little girl after such a traumatic event.

We headed back to the hotel and revisited the events of the day. All in all, it was a good day. The mule ride was exhilarating, the views outstanding and the sunset beyond description. It was hard to take it all in. Yet one moment of decision caused fear that was difficult to overcome, fear that froze us into inaction and caused panic to well up in me and my daughter.

Like Nadine did in that scary place, we must fix our eyes on our Father. Don't look left or right, don't look up or down, but set your gaze on the source of your hope; Jesus. Don't look away. He is absolutely trustworthy to see you through every circumstance of this life and he will be there at your last breath to escort you into His presence. Amazing! Are your eyes fixed on Christ? Ask God to sustain you. He will.

Hebrews 12:1-2a NIV

[1] *Therefore, since we are surrounded by such a great cloud of witnesses, let us throw off everything that hinders and the sin that so easily entangles. And let us run with perseverance the race marked out for us,* [2] *fixing our eyes on Jesus, the pioneer and perfecter of faith.*

Deadman Pass
White Out!

My wife Becky and I, along with our five children, a dog and our cat were driving down a highway in eastern Oregon singing at the top of our lungs. Actually only five of us were singing; our twin daughters, only six months old and strapped snuggly in their car seats, were looking at us like we were all daft...but who heeds the input of a six-month-old? They were the proverbial "peanut gallery."

The singing ensued after a fairly nerve-racking stretch of snow-covered road disappeared in my rearview mirror, having been outwitted by some careful driving and encouraging words. The seven of us were piled in a Ford conversion van complete with camper in tow. We were pointed west and headed where many dreams and hopes awaited us. The van was stuffed full of presents received from family and friends in Utah where we had spent the previous two weeks celebrating Christmas.

The song really was an attempt to ease our nerves and bring a little sunshine to a dreary, snowy day. I don't know how many of you have driven a van through a snowstorm, but they really aren't designed for such an adventure. The slipping left and right, the swaying of the camper and the sketchy roads all required a renewed effort of optimism and focus. Though it seemed we could see the freight train coming (metaphorically speaking) but couldn't get out of the way.

Our goal that day was the Columbia River Gorge, a beautiful area of river lined by majestic mountains, but first we had to get through Dead Man Pass, the connection from eastern to western Oregon along I-84; and aptly named. The drop-offs were extreme and the grades challenging. As we approached the pass near Meacham, Oregon, we realized the route was too steep and slippery to attempt without chains. I pulled the van over into a chain-up area and put on the cable chains I had purchased a few towns back. They slipped on, no thanks to my numb figures, and gave a positive feel to our progress up the mountain. I felt a little like the star of *Ice Road Truckers;* big rig crawling up the mountain, no possibility of turning around now, onward and upward!

Up the pass we went. It was snowing heavily, and traffic had crawled to a snail's pace. All around us was nothing but white and glare. The twins were finally asleep, and the rest of the kids were excited to be a part of such an adventure. I honestly can't tell you what my wife was thinking but I know I was very nervous.

Near the top of the pass the wind picked up, first a little and then intensely. In a moment, we were in a complete white-out from blowing snow. It happened so suddenly that I wasn't sure what to do. The visibility was zero. I couldn't even see the end of the hood of our van. I had no choice but to stop right where I was in the middle of the road, praying that no one would run into us.

The wind howled like nothing I'd experienced before. It was hitting the left side of our van and literally rocking it back and forth. We had a CB radio with us and heard the chatter from truckers up and down the pass. Everyone was experiencing the same thing we were. "I can't see my mirrors," one would say. "I'm stopped dead in the road," another would declare through the crackle and static of the signal.

"Well, at least we're not alone," I thought as I turned the fan up to give us more heat. The wind was so intense that it was sucking the heat from our van. Six-month-old twins, five children under ten, two animals and two adults crammed in a small space for what turned into hours. After about two of those hours, I noticed that the snow was piling up on the side of my door. It was a mere two feet below my windshield and growing. I'd heard of drifts that buried entire semis in the west and now, my thoughts turned to survival. I soon realized that in a few more hours we would be buried in a drift ourselves, and then it happened. The temperature light came on indicating the van was overheating.

"How could that be?" I thought. "It's fifteen degrees out!" Then I realized that the snow was blowing so hard it was freezing on the radiator, causing the problem. I thought about the prospect of seven people in freezing conditions and no heat at all! Sobering. I reacted. I knew I had to clear the radiator of ice or we were in big trouble. I told Becky what I had to do, put on every stitch of clothing I could find and pushed the driver's door open against the menacing drift.

The wind blew so hard that I was barely able to hold it open and step out. Immediately I grabbed the large side mirror and hung on against the gale. As I reached around the van with my left hand, holding onto the mirror with my right hand, I prayed to God. The situation was so intense that if the mirror had broken, I would have been blown many feet away from the vehicle. I reached under the bumper with the ice scraper that I was firmly grasping and began scraping. My face was freezing and my fingers going numb; much was at stake. A coating of slush and ice had built up on the radiator nearly three inches thick. With determined purpose I cleared the ice and worked my way back into the van. In only a few minutes, the fruit of my labor was realized; and the engine cooled down, eliminating the annoying light.

Heat once again flowed into the passenger area and the tension was eased somewhat. Twice in three hours, the wind let up just enough to see that we were parked right next to a streetlight, perhaps the entrance to a rest area, though I wasn't sure. We were sitting there contemplating what to do when a voice barked over the radio. It was a trucker and he said, "I'm going for it!" In the next instant the weather cleared enough that I could see about a foot past my front bumper, and then a chill ran down my spine. We could hear the truck, blowing his air horns, right behind us. I threw the van into drive anticipating a blow on my back bumper. Miraculously, the truck saw our brake lights and swerved a little to the left in time to miss us with only a foot or so of clearance on the driver's side. He was so close that his wheels knocked down the drift that had been creeping up my door.

I made an instantaneous decision to use the truck as our way out. As soon as I saw his back lights clear the front of the van, I gunned it. The van lurched and the chains bit. We managed to pull directly behind the truck and stay about ten feet away, following his every move. We were moving about 15-20 miles per hour and our position behind the truck had improved our visibility. Though we could now see, all we could see was the back doors and bumper of the 18-wheeler. That cat and mouse game went on for only a few minutes and we were out of it. The whiteout was only at the very summit of the pass and was no more than half a mile wide. As we emerged, it was clear, cold and inviting. We could see the city lights far below us and we thanked God for his merciful provision.

Many of you, right now, are sitting in the same van we sat in years ago. The wind is howling, things look hopeless and the options are few. The more you try to solve your dilemma, the more desperate it gets. You may have even come to a point where you have verbalized, "God, I'm ready **"What God sees is that the seemingly impossible circumstance you are in, like our white out, isn't very wide. It is a small part of a larger life that God, our Redeemer, has full control over."**

to go home. I can't make it in this situation." As impossible as things appear to you, I want to encourage you. Like a view on Google Maps, you see things at street level. If you would ask God to show you His perspective, things just a little like He sees them, it would give you renewed hope. Take your mouse, click on the zoom button and zoom out. What God sees is that the seemingly impossible circumstance you are in, like our white out, isn't very wide. It is a small part of a larger life that God, our Redeemer, has full control over. Ask Him for perspective. Ask Him for understanding and trust completely in His ability and desire to walk with you through the blinding storm.

I know with full assurance that God sent us that truck. I know that it was no accident that we heard it and he saw us. I know that if the truck was any further away, we would not have seen it and very likely have suffered great loss. I know that if the truck had been any closer, we would have been in a serious accident and also suffered great loss; yet it wasn't either of those things...it was perfect...because God ordained it so.

I encourage you, I exhort you, take your situation to God. Be genuine and honest. He is absolutely faithful to love you and preserve you through all eternity.

Isaiah 42:16 NIV

I will lead the blind by ways they have not known, along unfamiliar paths I will guide them; I will turn the darkness into light before them and make the rough places smooth. These are the things I will do; I will not forsake them.

From Death to Life

God's Eternal Plan

"If you plant them six inches apart, at about four inches deep and in rows separated by a foot or so, you will have great coverage and a healthy crop." The emaciated old farmer seemed to enjoy sharing his knowledge of planting corn. A greasy, torn straw hat dipped over his heavy brow concealing most of his left eye and proudly bore a chicken feather sticking from its band.

"And, if ya throw a little cow manure on top of the whole plot, along with lots of water, you'll have the best sweet corn you've ever eaten come about the first week of August. I suggest the Sweet Ambrosia seed here," he said chewing on a piece of timothy grass. It looked like he had planted many crops over the years, so I handed him a twenty-dollar bill and secured my purchase in the back seat.

We had recently purchased a home in the country with three-and a-half acres and I was anxious to begin a large garden plot. "Providing for your family, now that's what it's all about," I thought as I pulled into our gravel drive. To me that meant the biggest garden plot I could possibly manage; pumpkins, corn, tomatoes, peppers, string beans, snap peas, radishes, carrots, potatoes, fresh herbs, squash, and a myriad of other produce that would provide for our family through the long winter ahead. I fired up the rotor-tiller I'd borrowed and began cutting into the earth with the rotating blades.

I soon found the machine was a hard beast to tame! The constant vibration and beating of the tiller wrenched my back so hard it became painful. I'd thought it would be easier. One day into it and I had to ask a friend to finish the work. I was laid up. I attacked the farming challenge like a race car with no fuel; I never left the starting line.

With a lot of help from my wife and children, we managed to put in the crop. Row after row of plants went in with great expectation of the harvest, and then we waited, and waited, and waited. It seemed forever until the first green sprouts pushed their way through the soil to be embraced by the warm sun; first the radishes and finally the corn. Over those many days of waiting, I wondered if the crops would ever produce fruit. After they emerged, they were pretty scrawny. Little wisps of plants that I could easily flick with my finger and uproot, yet over time they began to grow larger.

After about eight weeks, the tomato plants were monoliths covering a large section of the garden. I thought, "If one tomato plant is good, fifteen are better!" Suffice it to say that describing the tomato harvest in bushels was inadequate. The other plants also flourished growing slowly at first, then filling out quickly. It's as if we waited forever to see them for the first time, and then they grew at such a rate that it was astonishing. The harvesting process that year was long and tiring. I have never seen so much food produced from a garden we'd planted. It seemed that every condition was right, and God multiplied our efforts ten-fold. Every Sunday throughout the late summer and early fall, we'd take bags of food to church giving them to those in need.

One day as I was harvesting some veggies, I thought of the amazing plan God has for each of us; to bring us from death to life, and of the way He plants his Word in our hearts to bear fruit for His kingdom. What a mysterious thing. It is only after a plant blossoms that a seed is produced, seemingly dead. Yet if that seed is put into the right environment, surrounded by moisture, soil and nutrients, it is brought to life eventually growing into a strong plant that bears fruit. Yet if that seed is placed into the wrong environment, such as on a sidewalk, it will wither and die.

We are much like that seed. If we die to ourselves and embrace the Living Word of God, we will be nourished and bear fruit, however, if we walk a path that somehow minimizes or discounts God, we are already dead spiritually and will simply "exist" until our physical death.

> **"If we die to ourselves and embrace the Living Word of God, we will be nourished and bear fruit…"**

For it is God who imagined us, God who created us, God who imbued us with specific gifts, temperaments and talents, and it is God who will sustain us through His Spirit and Living Word with a new life in Christ.

The next time you plant a garden, remember the Author of Life. He is the Great Gardener. Those who are pruned by his shears are blessed.

John 15:1-4 NIV

[1]"I am the true vine, and my Father is the gardener. [2]He cuts off every branch in me that bears no fruit, while every branch that does bear fruit, he prunes so that it will be even more fruitful. [3]You are already clean because of the word I have spoken to you. [4]Remain in me, and I will remain in you. No branch can bear fruit by itself; it must remain in the vine. Neither can you bear fruit unless you remain in me.

Losing my Mind

A Life of Distractions

Somewhere in the span of the last 30 years, I lost my mind. I seem to remember having it with me when I left Denver on a South West flight but can't remember if I carried it off of the plane or not. I know I packed it but can't remember if I pulled it out to use on the long flight. It's probably still in the seat-back pocket in the row where I was sitting. Well, I hope if someone finds it, they can use it. I don't think it had a nametag so there's little hope of getting it back.

Have you ever lost something and panicked? Perhaps your cell phone slipped out of your pocket settling into the cushions of your couch. Then in the short span of one hour the battery died so that it wouldn't ring when you called it. The chance of finding it is slim unless you move the couch to a new location.

Or you put your credit cards in your wallet, laid your wallet down, ran upstairs to brush your teeth and ran out the door to work forgetting to pick it up. About noon you headed to Chick-fil-A, ordered a #7 with a diet coke, reached in your pocket for money and realized that little flap of fabric was empty. No wallet. Embarrassing! Then you retraced your steps remembering that you laid the wallet on a table in the living room.

Oh, and It didn't stop there. By the time you arrived home, one of your children in an unusual fit of guilt decided to pick up the living room as a kind gesture, except children trying to be kind rarely do things right; but certainly, they do them quickly. As your darling child flew through the living room, your wallet (sitting in plain sight) was tossed into a paper bag, along with anything else that would fit, and was stuffed in a closet. Of course, looking at the time, they realized they were late to soccer practice and ran out the door. Then you arrived home to grab your wallet so that you could go buy some groceries, but your wallet wasn't there, and you began questioning your sanity and retracing your steps again. Sound familiar?

Well, if I wrote a story about my life, the parallels would be astonishing, except it may be my mind that was stuffed in the paper bag instead of my wallet! Day in, day out we place ourselves in a routine that is stressful, emotional and often chaotic.

Our lives and heads become so full of "things" that we can't think clearly about any of them. We try to sort them and stuff them in the various compartments of our minds, but they are like so many ants flowing from an ant hill; they find their way out. The overflow of our minds has no place to settle. How is it we let our lives get to that point? We take on so much that we neglect basic housekeeping and our brains become cluttered, forgetting things critically important to us. God did not create us to be busy, though within reason, we need to have things to do. God did, however, create us to be in fellowship with him.

What keeps you from communing with the Father? What keeps you so busy and distracted? Sometimes we fill our lives and minds with things because there is a great void that needs to be filled; pain, fear or loneliness. Sometimes we fill them because we don't think anyone can accomplish a task better than we can, and sometimes we fill them because it distracts us from other deeply difficult issues and problems in our lives.

Let me assure you that God is greater than anything that comes into your life, no matter how desperate it may seem. We are not told to fill our lives and minds with clutter, rather we are told to "be still, and know that I am God."

"We are not told to fill our lives and minds with clutter, rather we are told to "be still, and know that I am God."

That is an uncomfortable place for many; being still. It's in the stillness that we see ourselves as we really are. It's in the stillness that we can hear the voice of God. It's in the stillness that we are able to clear our minds and know that God is with us; and when we know that God loves us and adores us, we understand better the beauty and importance of the sacrifice of Jesus Christ.

Oh God, teach me your ways. Lead me down the path of righteousness. Then I will sing your praises. Then I will be at peace.

Psalm 42:10-11 NIV

[10] "Be still and know that I am God; I will be exalted among the nations, I will be exalted in the earth." [11] The LORD Almighty is with us; the God of Jacob is our fortress. Selah

-Day 16-

To the Summit!

The Purpose and Value of Life

Notwithstanding the audible gasps for oxygen in the thin air at 10,000 feet, the collective impact of a mountain-top vista on the psyche of any individual taking in such a spectacle cannot be measured by human means. The spiritual and mental refreshment that comes from viewing mountain peaks, distant rainstorms, seas of green conifers contrasted by deep shadows, and silver ribbons of water glistening on the valley floors is nothing short of exhilarating. Add to that the unimaginable varied colors of the sky filled with clouds rolling by overhead and you have a glimpse of what it may be like in heaven.

That is where I found myself that cool September afternoon in the mountains above Salt Lake City, sitting on a boulder high above the bustle and taking in the grandeur of God's creation. I had started out early that morning on a solo hike to the top of Mt. Olympus. The mountain loomed above the valley floor and ascended steeply to its rocky peak. It challenged nearly anyone who trudged up the tiny trail that leads to the top because of its pitch. Pitch is simply a measure of rise compared to run, or in simpler terms, a measure of "steepness."

Mt Olympus is only 4.2 miles to the summit, a relatively short hike, yet it rises nearly 4600 feet from the beginning of the climb. What that means is that it gains about 1000 feet per mile, rarely providing a flat spot for a respite. I had set out to climb the mountain for my dad, actually my father-in-law. He had reached his early eighties and was no longer able to climb mountains as he used to. Most of his life he had been buff and spent many, many hours on the mountains and trails above Salt Lake City, and Mt. Olympus was one of his favorites.

"Now when you get to the creek, you're about one-third of the way up. If you think it was steep to that point, hang on, because then it really gets steep!" I remember the words as if it was yesterday.

"Dad," I said "I'm going to climb this mountain for you, even though I'm not sure I can make it to the top. If I do, I'll take lots of pictures and bring them back for you." Even as I said the words, I doubted I could reach the summit. I wasn't young myself and the task ahead was a nearly impossible one. Even if I made it to the cirque, the last 800 feet were straight up, climbing a nearly vertical wall that had defeated many before me.

"You can do it son," he said to me reminiscing about the many times he had covered the same ground. "When you near the top it will be very windy. Hold onto the rocks firmly, it's a long drop!"

I loaded my daypack with everything I would need for the hike; rain gear, sunscreen, water, water filter, Power Bars, and dry socks. I threw everything in the back of my car and headed to the trailhead. The morning air was crisp, and the weather was in my favor. As I attacked the first mile, sunlight spilled over the mountain peaks warming the frosty ground. Long streams of condensation formed around the warm air forcefully exiting my lungs. I thought about days gone by when such an occurrence would result in me stating, "Look mommy, I can see my breath." As it was, I looked more like a bull snorting and ready to charge.

When I arrived at the creek, the air was even cooler. The stream flowed down the mountainside and formed a little pool under some fir trees where the trail crossed. The combination of shade and air movement caused such a drop-in temperature, that I quickly moved on. Dad was right, the trail became really steep after that. Step by step I gained altitude, at times having to balance myself with one hand against the mountain. I remember sweating profusely and the perspiration making me cold, yet slowly I was beating the mountain. About a half mile before the cirque, I ran into two hikers coming down that had started before dawn and were now headed for the trailhead. As we passed, I said, "This is a lot of work for a Saturday morning!" They greeted me graciously and we spent a few minutes talking about the challenges of the hike.

When I arrived at the cirque I was dumbfounded. I don't believe I've ever seen a scene so raw yet so beautiful in my life. The definition of a cirque is basically a dead-end canyon. This one ended in nearly a 1000-foot wall made up of contorted, twisted rock, and I was standing on top of it. Wow! It caused my heart to skip a beat, and right there I began to worship God. What an amazing sight! What an amazing God!

I headed through the aspen finding the final climb to the summit; 800 feet of "straight up." Carefully I worked my way through the rocks and found myself on top, only thirty minutes after I started the final climb. I had to hop from rock to rock (the drop-offs between were too extreme to crawl down, then back up) finally making it to the summit. There, another sight greeted me; a nearly 2500-foot shear drop off. The wilderness spread out before me and the wind gently tugged at my jacket. Not the gale I was expecting and not the view I was expecting. I had anticipated looking over the Salt Lake Valley on the summit. Though I could glimpse sections of it, most of that view was blocked by rock. Instead I was able to peer out over a vast expanse of mountain peaks and wilderness to the east; awesome!

After a few moments I remembered why I was there - for dad. I began taking pictures trying to capture every possible angle. Then I pulled out my cell phone and was a little surprised to have a signal. I called him.

"Hello," I heard on the other end. "Who's this?"

"It's me, dad, Shannon."

"Shannon? This can't be Shannon; he's out climbing Mt. Olympus right now."

"It's me, dad, I'm standing on the summit of Mt. Olympus, and I wanted to tell you about the view I'm seeing right now!"

"Listen, I don't know who you are," he said, "but I know you're not Shannon. No phone could reach up there. There's no wire long enough!"

In a moment I realized that my father-in-law, in his 80's, had no concept of cell phones. He actually thought a phone wire had to be connected in order to talk to each other. It took me several minutes of persuading to convince him it was me and that phone signals could travel through the air. After my call, I spent another hour on the summit, ate a Power Bar and then headed down. Several weeks later I loaded the slide projector with my slides (yes, I used film!) and showed Dad the journey I had taken. He was thrilled and talked over and over about sights he had seen in the past on that mountain.

It was only a few years later that Dad had to move from our home where he had resided for eight years, and into an assisted living center. That transition helped me understand that every day we have with someone is a gift from God.

It is sobering to think back on the challenging hike and the purpose of climbing Mt. Olympus. Though personal blessing arose from the activity, the climb really was made to support my father-in-law. Each of us is truly blessed in so many ways by our Creator. We have been given our health, homes, family, and friends. Each of these is given to us for a short time and we are entrusted with them. We are stewards.

The longer I walk with Christ, the more blurred the line becomes between heaven and earth. I am here on earth, yet the spiritual is so real to me it's almost palpable. I work in ministry, yet my allegiance and purpose are in Christ. I find myself longing, like the deer in Psalm 42, for the face of God; to abide with him. I don't know what impact climbing that mountain for Dad had on him, but I clearly remember the flicker of joy that bounced in his eyes as we conversed about the adventure. And I don't know what impact my life has on those around me, yet I know there is one.

"Because we have been loved by God, we can now love others."

God is faithful. He tells us in his word that because we have been loved by him, we can now love others. That love of God then flows from us into the lives of others. Take a moment today to encourage someone you know. Build them up in the Lord for they are in our lives for only a short time, and we are privileged to be in theirs.

Luke 10:27 NIV

²⁷ He answered, "'Love the Lord your God with all your heart and with all your soul and with all your strength and with all your mind'; and, 'Love your neighbor as yourself.'"

-Day 17-

Observations in Nature

Worshiping the Creator

As we traveled over spring break, first to Jamestown and then to Washington D.C., spring was in full over-drive. The cherry blossoms were beaming radiantly in the splendor of their fresh pedals, the redbud added a pink splash of color to the forest undergrowth, and the dogwoods were laden with daisy-like blooms clothed in a creamy white dressing. Everywhere we looked, flowers and leaves were sprouting in abundance.

Normally I would drive by these sights and say something like, "Oh, that's pretty," but this time a question came to my mind. "Why do trees flower?" and "Why do flowers bloom?" While contemplating these questions it came to me that there may be many reasons why, but ultimately, they bloom because God created them that way. He designed them to open their blooms in spring, to bear fruit in season, to put oxygen into the air, to take carbon dioxide out of it, and to reproduce. He put them there to honor Him through their lives.

To that end, I realized that every living thing that fulfills God's intended purpose through its life, is really worshipping the Creator. When a tree is loaded with heavy blossoms bending its branches toward the earth, it's worshipping God. When a flower pokes through the soil and adorns itself with the beauty of a rosebud, it's worshiping God. When we purify our hearts in contrition and humility, we too are worshipping God.

I love Psalm 150. It ends by saying, "Let everything that has breath, praise the Lord!" For He is worthy of all honor and praise. We were created to worship God and to enjoy him forever. Fellowship and praise are our intended purpose. That's not a difficult job description, yet we complicate our relationship with God by adding all sorts of rules and requirements. We confuse love with performance and holiness with expectation. We become character assassins instead of thankful sheep. We openly state, "God could never love me," or "God requires more than I can give," instead of trusting him.

> **"We were created to worship God and to enjoy him forever. Fellowship and praise are our intended purpose."**

God is not demanding and waiting to chastise you for the slightest ill-conceived action. No. He simply asks us to love Him, a command that benefits us. And He promises to dwell with us, and love us, and protect us from the evil one.

Isaiah says, "The train of his (God's) robe filled the temple." Do you want to know an amazing truth? His temple is not some faraway place. It's not even on the other side of town. If you are His and have accepted His free gift of salvation through Jesus Christ, *you* are His temple! You are where He dwells; a holy place and a holy people.

Imagine, living with the Holy God inside of you and worshipping Him through your every thought and action. We are a privileged people; a people blessed by the Creator. May your life so reflect your love of God, that your very life is an act of worship.

Isaiah 6:1-3 NIV

¹I saw the Lord seated on a throne, high and exalted, and the train of his robe filled the temple. ² Above him were seraphs, each with six wings: With two wings they covered their faces, with two they covered their feet, and with two they were flying. ³ And they were calling to one another: "Holy, holy, holy is the LORD Almighty; the whole earth is full of his glory."

A Day on the Farm
Reflections

For a brief period in my life I managed a Christmas tree farm. It sat on 80 acres of woods and fields, holding 85,000 Christmas trees. I loved the job. Though physically taxing, daily I was in the woods and communing with God in nature; one of my favorite things.

The entrance to the farm was a steep graded road plowed into the ground of the surrounding oak forest. The drive was about a half mile long and so steep that two "thank-you-mam's" were cut into it. A "thank-you-mam" is a place that is level along a steep grade offering additional traction and relief from an intimidating ascent. Encountering such a spot of security going up a hill provides so much "emotional relief" that they are called "thank-you-mam's", as in, thank you for the sure footing or break from having to concentrate so hard.

The road proved to be a significant obstacle for many of the semis that climbed to our farm for a load of trees. The trucks always towed large trailers that would hold as many as 500 trees if properly bundled and stacked. One particularly new and shiny truck entered our road and lost traction part way up. The Kenworth, spit polished to the hilt, began slinging mud from the soupy mess on the hill and soon covered nearly every inch of the vehicle with an oozy brown mixture of water, dirt and detritus. Feeling especially bad for the driver I ran to get my 1950's Farm-All tractor, a throw back from an era long past. The back tires were huge, but the front tires were tiny and set closely together giving the effect of a tricycle.

I backed down the road toward the mired truck stopping ten feet short of its position. The trucker had already connected a stout chain to his front bumper and dragged the other end to be connected to the tractor. After he wrapped the chain around the Farm-All's frame, I tightened the slack and gave him a heads-up which he could clearly see from his new position inside the cab. I shoved it into low gear and pulled back the throttle releasing all 24 horses in a mighty leap.

The back wheels of the tractor began to spin in the mud, but headway slowly was made as the trucker gunned his engine as well. The sight was one for the record books. My tiny little red tractor crawling up the hill pulling a sixty-foot multi-ton behemoth complete with sleeper cab! After achieving the summit, a sight unfolded that still cheers my soul to think about. The tree farm was buzzing; literally.

The migrant workers we hired every fall were actively harvesting trees all around us. Trees were being cut with a tool called a Bachtold. It basically looks like a high-wheeled brush mower, only it wields a 28" saw blade instead of a mower blade. The blade was unprotected in the front. All a worker had to do was "bump" a Christmas tree with the blade and it would cut through the trunk, felling it. Rows and rows of trees were falling all around us as another group of workers, led by a tractor pulling a bailer, shoved the harvested trees through the machine which wound them tightly into a bundle. The maneuver compressed the trees to only one-third their original size making it possible to ship more on a single truck.

The truckers coming to our farm always represented a buyer and they would pay cash for the trees. Often, I would have many thousands of dollars wadded up in my pocket from the transactions and never gave thought to the possibility of theft. It was a different era, or perhaps I was short sighted. The trees were loaded onto a stake-bed wagon that was pulled by another tractor behind the bailer. The wagons were taken to the waiting semis where they were loaded by a crew of men stationed at the rigs. The trees were manually tossed from the wagon to the semi-trailers and neatly stacked for their ride to the retailer that had purchased them.

"I realized even then that apart from God there is no beauty and no sculpted landscapes."

As I look back on my experience on the tree farm, I become a little emotional. It was a beautiful place that stirred my soul. I even remember asking God to provide it someday in the future as a Christian camp. In my mind I could see kids working on the farm, studying God's word and learning life skills. As far as I know, that never came to be, though I haven't been back to the farm for thirty years.

Probably my favorite memory was after the bustle of the day, sitting quietly on a stump and watching the sun drop below the tree line. It didn't matter the time of year; it was always a sight to see. I would often sit on that stump and thank God for his hand on my life and on the lives of my wife and children. I realized even then that apart from God there is no beauty or no sculpted landscapes. Without Him the trees would not draw nutrients from the soil, or power from the sun to grow and replenish the oxygen we breathe. Without Him there would be no squirrels running around the treetops, chattering at deer below and cutting the nuts that drop to the ground. Our God is amazing. He completely provides everything we need. He is the Source of Life.

Take a moment, find a stump and sit on it. Watch a sunset, smell the sweet odor of the forest, hear the chatter of the animals who call it home, and thank God in that quiet place for loving you.

Acts 17: 24-28 NIV

[24]"The God who made the world and everything in it is the Lord of heaven and earth and does not live in temples built by hands. [25]And he is not served by human hands, as if he needed anything, because he himself gives all men life and breath and everything else. [26]From one man he made every nation of men, that they should inhabit the whole earth; and he determined the times set for them and the exact places where they should live. [27]God did this so that men would seek him and perhaps reach out for him and find him, though he is not far from each one of us. [28]'For in him we live and move and have our being.' As some of your own poets have said, 'We are his offspring.'

A Mighty Leap

The Pain of Sin

"Jump, it's only three feet. You can make it!" The words of encouragement were coming from my hiking partner Alex as I stared at a void dropping nearly three hundred feet down. The void opened to the desert floor below. The route we chose required jumping three feet onto a section of sloping red-rock inviting us from the other side. If the ground were two feet below us the maneuver would have been easy but staring into the depths unnerved me. "Jump? Are you running on all cylinders, Alex?" In a flash he ran past me, took a mighty leap, and landed on the other side.

The morning was cool as the sun began to warm the tops of red spires scattered throughout the beautiful canyon country before us. We had been planning this trip to the Maze area of Canyonlands for many months. The deeply cut canyons ran in all directions, forming a maze that swallowed you up without proper maps and orienteering gear. We were standing on top of the canyons near our campsite, looking into the vast expanse of eroded sandstone and layered rocks.

The only way into the Maze was along a 31 mile stretch of dirt road culminating in a "nail-biting" descent down a 1200-foot cliff to the area we were camping. The road cut into the side of the cliff seemed to hang onto little more than thin air. It was barely the width of our truck and was riddled with boulders, some as large as three feet across. One tire would roll over a rock tipping us precariously toward the edge, and then right us as level footing again was found. We drove down one section of road, jockeyed the truck around a switchback, and then drove down the next section. This pattern was repeated at least nine times before we rolled through a dry creek bed at the bottom.

The beauty that greeted us in the Maze was astounding. The intricate slot canyons, the multiple hues of red painted into the rocks, the large expanses of country, and the deep contrasting colors of green from the scattered junipers were a sight to behold. It is some of the most inspiring country in the world!

The jump was necessary to access the trailhead into the area we had scouted out on our map. Our goal that day was the *Great Gallery*, a very large panel of Anasazi petroglyphs in one of the canyons in the Maze. The hike from our campsite to the canyon floor required an eight-hundred-foot climb down and the jump was near the beginning of our descent. I mustered all of the resolve I could and made a flying leap toward the other side. The heavy daypack I was carrying pulled me backward just enough to cause a landing six inches short of my goal. Alex reached out and grabbed my hand pulling me away from a painful end as I praised his efforts profusely.

When we reached the bottom, we noticed a large area filled with water; a rare sight in that part of the desert. The pond had formed in the bottom of a streambed filled from the rain that fell the night before. The water stretched over fifty feet in length and was two feet deep. We stopped to pump some of the water through our filters to top off our water bladders and to explore the banks for any sign of animals. The water was cool and sweet, testifying to the pristine area we were in.

We followed the streambed for a while, as it was on our route, and came across two very small pools less than three feet across. They were situated under a large overhang that shaded them from the intense sun frequenting this area in the summer. It was obvious that these pools were sustained year-round, evidenced by the large Yucca plants growing around them. Yuccas are a member of the Agave family and sport needle-sharp leaves that help to protect them from marauding herbivores. They tend to grow in places that have limited moisture content in the soil, storing much of that moisture in their long, thin leaves.

The pools also supported a small population of frogs - an unusual animal in such an arid place. As we studied the pools, we saw something that took us a while to understand. Before us was a small frog impaled on one of the Yucca leaves. For some reason he had decided it was time to go from one pool to the other. Rather than slowly hopping along the ground, he took a mighty leap (much like our jump earlier) launching himself nearly three feet into the air, except he never made it. Between him and his goal was one of those long, sharp Yucca leaves and there he hung, dried up and shriveled, skewered through the abdomen and still hanging on the tip of a Yucca leaf. Now that was a bad day!

As I studied the frog that met its demise on the end of a Yucca plant, I realized that the plant likely wasn't even a consideration as the amphibian eyed the second pool. It simply was part of the surroundings the frog lived in. It was something the frog was accustomed to. Though it grew from a small plant into something large, it went unnoticed.

In a similar way, sin can creep into our lives, first starting as something small, yet little by little growing into something large. Something life threatening. Unchecked, it can take on the characteristics of a monster, tearing at the very fiber of our being. Or like the frog, cause great pain, and change your life as you know it. Take a moment and ask God to show you the giant Yucca plant in your life and then ask him to weed it out. For you are His, bought with a price and sealed for redemption. May peace abound in your life. Should you see the King before me, well, I'll be a little jealous.

Psalm 1:1-3 NIV

[1] *Blessed is the man who does not walk in the counsel of the wicked or stand in the way of sinners or sit in the seat of mockers.* [2] *But his delight is in the law of the LORD, and on his law he meditates day and night.* [3] *He is like a tree planted by streams of water, which yields its fruit in season and whose leaf does not wither. Whatever he does prospers.*

The Most Secure Investment
Our Eyes on Eternity

In a world of volatile stock prices, corporate failures and the loss of huge amounts of retirement income, it is good to know that there is a secure investment that will never lose value or cause regret once you've made it: **people.**

Throughout my high school years, I fashioned myself a mountain man. So enamored was I with the idea of trekking through limitless wilderness, living off the land and sucking in long draughts of crisp mountain air that I pursued jobs in the northwest as I was nearing graduation. I wanted to be in Alaska or the Yukon so bad I could taste it. Obedient to the urge, I began looking in outdoor magazines for potential job opportunities in that area of our continent. (No internet, or even personal computers then!) Rationalizing that many people would be happy to have a strapping young energetic lad working for them, I wrote two letters to potential employers: one was a hunting guide in Alaska, and the other a fishing boat captain, and they both responded.

As I received my first reply in the mail, I envisioned the red-carpet royalty treatment. "Yes Mr. Dare, we would be happy to have a strapping young energetic lad like you employed in our firm. We will move your things and book you on our private jet to Alaska where you will be met by awe-struck employees of our firm who will coddle you and meet your every need." I thought how at eighteen I had finally made it. Why, they'll move me to Alaska, I'll work a few months to finance an outfit and then be off, headed for the freedom of the wilderness!

As I read the response from the hunting guide, it became clear that my expectations were a little high. He stated that he would be happy to have me in his camp but only for the summer. During that time, he would trade work for food, board and experience. (There went my outfit!) My responsibilities would be to help drag the dead animals up or down the mountains after his clients made the perfect shot, frequently carry a minimum of 100lb loads of meat, and to deal with other nasty odd jobs around camp including latrine duty. Finally, he said, "Let me know if you're coming and when you'll be here. If you can't find a ride, hiking will eventually get you to my camp."

I was so out of focus that I actually considered his offer. "I'll wait until I hear from the boat captain," I thought, "Perhaps he'll make me a better offer." I didn't know it at the time, but I could easily have been on an episode of Most Dangerous Catch had the show been airing then. When I did hear from the boat captain, he asked me to come to western Canada to talk with him. He ran a fish processing boat that used enormous nets to take in cod and other fish, clean them and prepare them for commercial sale. Again, no flight to the northwest. No real offer, just a chance.

As I reflect on the two opportunities, I realize the reason I didn't point myself west and thumb my way to a new future was because of the thought of labor, and blood, and fish, and rocking boats, and more labor. At that time in my life, I had an aversion to labor. I added the equations presented and couldn't come up with Daniel Boone in the Alaskan wild, so I declined them both.

Very disappointed and still smack-dab in the center of the corn-belt of the U.S., I decided a summer job more locally was a good idea. Instead of my Daniel Boone outfit I set my sights on two things: purchasing a motorcycle and a rifle. I didn't care if they were both old and rusty as long as they worked. I reasoned that I could strap my rifle to the back of my bike, load up some grub and just drive to the northwest where I could live happily off the land, forever. I found a job at a trailer factory to fund my dream.

That factory built large A class RV's. As the wheeled chassis rolled down the assembly line, a man jumped into the half-built units and drilled holes for the pedestals holding both the driver's seat and passenger's seat. My job was to bolt those pedestals onto the RV frame. As I did this, an electrician wired the computer and vehicle harness into the camper. Unbeknown to me, God placed Wayne in my life. Wayne was an apostolic preacher who worked during the day and preached in the evenings and on Sundays. He was the electrician.

Though I was raised in a great family, I was a little hostile toward openly professing Christians. From the first moment we met, Wayne began telling me about Jesus. He would wire away as I reached under the frame to find where the bolts would slip through, and he would share about his Jesus. I became pretty good at judging the 7.5 inches the bolts were separated by, and he became very good at seeing my heart. I openly challenged him time after time, yet I came to enjoy those conversations. He was so well versed in the Scriptures that I struggled to find a question he couldn't answer about the Bible. I would go home and read the Bible just to find some obscure fact or question that I thought he couldn't answer. I remember looking forward to the day I would gain the upper hand. All summer I continued with the same pattern; read, find a little-known fact, challenge Wayne.

Now let me say that God definitely has a sense of humor because as I read and read, his word began to permeate my heart. Over a period of months involving Wayne's patience and testimony, and scripture reading, I saw God's great gift and plan for my life. One evening, at Wayne's church God saved my life. My eyes were opened to my condition and my eternal soul had a new promise of peace. I headed to Utah for college that fall, helping me a little with my outdoor desires, and have never seen Wayne since.

God directed my life that summer putting me in the presence of a man that loved me and had my eternal life as his focus. I was someone he didn't know, someone he could have avoided, and someone that needed him worse

"Wayne was obedient to the call of the Savior; investing his earthly days in the lives of those God put in his path. Now that is an investment that will never fail, or lose value, or disappear."

than he needed me. Wayne was obedient to the call of the Savior; investing his earthly days in the lives of those God put in his path. Now that is an investment that will never fail, or lose value, or disappear. You see, that act of kindness has impacted many. Each of our lives impact the world in ways we can never imagine. How would the world be different if you never spoke into the life of another, or if you never ministered to your family? Might I say, very different?

We are called to be salt and light to a desperate and fallen world around us. We have been given a great inheritance; we are sons of God. We are called to mercy, and to care about the eternal condition of everyone God connects us to. May you be obedient to that call. May you share yourself with the needy, with the destitute and with the lowly, for you were such as these before Christ transformed you into a radiant being; into a child of the King.

Romans 12:1-2 NIV

[1]Therefore, I urge you, brothers, in view of God's mercy, to offer your bodies as living sacrifices, holy and pleasing to God—this is your spiritual act of worship. [2]Do not conform any longer to the pattern of this world but be transformed by the renewing of your mind. Then you will be able to test and approve what God's will is—his good, pleasing and perfect will.

Your word is a lamp for my feet, a light on my path. Psalm 119:105 NIV

-Day 21-

Surrender your Life

Freedom through the Cross

Fear gripped me as I looked into the eyes of the great menace confronting me. The eyes of the beast were dark with streaks of red permeating the normally white cornea. Heavy brows formed an ominous furrow on the forehead of the peril at hand, and I'm sure I saw drops of saliva form around its lips. Instantaneously I reacted crouching to a defensive position but found myself in a corner that was tough to get out of. Panic ensued as I weighed my options, looking about for any means of escape.

"Shannon," I heard as my eyes landed on an open door. I quickly calculated the needed velocity to make it through unscathed. "Shannon, did you hear me?" Mr. Bower, my elementary principal, asked.

Mr. Bower was a topic of discussion among all of the third graders at my school. Ever since kindergarten, I had heard of the "principal's office," a dark place where very few students emerged after entering. I imagined what might have happened to all of those students as I attended first and second grade. Likely they were still there being interrogated by the principal.

"Shannon, why did you yell out during the spelling bee?" Mr. Bower demanded taking his cue from Mrs. Smith, my third-grade teacher. My mind was finally forced to the brutal reality of my situation. I answered, "Because I didn't want to spell the words."

"And why didn't you want to spell the words?" he asked.

"Because I didn't study," I answered running through the potential outcomes of my interrogation. Though not a student of history, I remembered learning about interrogators. They are able to discern even a twitch in the corner of your eye and deduce your level of guilt.

"Shannon, do you understand that it is inappropriate to yell out in class like that?" Mr. Bower queried.

"Yes," I answered, not knowing any other response at the time.

"You know we'll need to call your mother and let her know about this," he said. "After I talk with her, I'll ask you to come back to the office."

"I took Mrs. Smith's hand and walked solemnly back to my classroom, slumping into my seat. There the students looked at me like I had just stolen a national treasure. In retrospect, I really didn't mind spelling bees; I was just a victim of overactive child syndrome. To this day I blame my mother for feeding me a jelly doughnut and a glass of chocolate milk for breakfast that morning.

As the year progressed, I found myself disliking school more and more. Even the thought of going to school caused headaches and symptoms of nausea. I found myself going to school fearful of what might happen that day. After a while I realized the problem was a lack of closure. Even though I had survived the initial confrontation with Mr. Bower, he never called my mother. For months I lived in fear that he would finally call mom and tell her of my criminal activity, but he didn't. I suffered a fate far worse than reality; I suffered from a lack of completing an important emotional process in my life.

I guess I could have confessed my outburst to mom, but the thought never really crossed my mind. Instead of confronting the situation, I lived in fear, and it grew by leaps and bounds. My thoughts manifested

"I believe the enemy has used this one singular tool (fear) to incapacitate the Christian people of our nation. Fear strips you of confidence, of optimism and of hope. It migrates to the very center of your being, spreading lie after lie."

outcomes like the uncertainty that confronts you in a dark, damp basement; irrational and damaging. Nowhere is it written that a dark damp basement has some hidden menace, and nowhere is it written that we must live in fear. In fact, Christ has set us free from fear through the power and promise of his blood.

What I experienced in third grade is that fear is debilitating. It will take the fullness of who you are and strip you down to a shell of that person. It's not much different from cancer except, rather than growing in our tissues, it grows in our minds to write a reality that didn't exist before. I believe the enemy has used this one singular tool to incapacitate the Christian people of our nation. Fear strips you of confidence, of optimism and of hope. It migrates to the very center of your being, spreading lie after lie.

Now we are faced with a brutal reality; that we fear because we fail to trust. We imagine our future and all that the world may pack into it, yet we easily remove God from the equation. Somehow that part of the story is pushed to an inaccessible compartment of our mind where it is discounted or forgotten. We live with both feet in the world and forsake the Author of Life.

What is amazing is that we would choose to give up the blessings of an intimate relationship with Jesus. If we go back to my third-grade year, a simple confession would have brought understanding, compassion, and encouragement. And I wouldn't have spent months in fear. How much more with Jesus? Obedience and trust, even a little, will be blessed by God beyond our ability to comprehend. Refusing to trust God is like knowing there is a wonderful present under the Christmas tree, and because we're trying to make a point, we decline to open it. The negative consequences are ours; belonging to no one else.

I believe, much like fear is the singular thing crippling the Christian nation, the singular thing to combat fear is surrender. We must give our futures to God, knowing no matter how our future is written, it is His. And He is faithful to secure that future for His glory and honor.

Proverbs 3:1-3 NIV
[1] My son, do not forget my teaching, but keep my commands in your heart, [2] for they will prolong your life many years and bring you prosperity. [3] Let love and faithfulness never leave you; bind them around your neck, write them on the tablet of your heart.

-Day 22-

Believing God

His Light in Dark Places

All right, it's no secret, I'm an *outdoor-aholic* – no question. I would have sought help for it years ago but I ran into a problem. I asked our insurance carrier if they would cover treatments, but they told me that anyone who spent as much time in the wilderness as I did, in the dangerous conditions I often encountered, was just plain crazy. Then they told me there was no coverage because craziness was a pre-existing condition; so here I am, still passionately pursuing the outdoors with no insurance to help.

Let me share an example with you. In high school, I decided that spelunking (caving) was something I wanted to try. Eventually I became hooked on it. One of my favorite things to do was to repel down a completely black 150 foot pit, jump off of the rope into 3 feet of mud, squeeze my ample body into the tiniest hole I could find, crawl some undetermined distance using my toes and elbows, and pop out into a cavern far beneath the earth.

Let me stop and say that God has spared me over and over again from an early demise. It's like I had no concept of pain or suffering. Whatever the challenge, I would jump in both feet first with full assurance in myself and my own abilities.

I grew up in Northern Indiana, a great place for corn, soybeans and fishing, but not a very good place to find caves, in fact there were none. After months of looking, I found a group of zealots as crazy as me and we began driving on the weekends to southern Indiana where caves were numerous. The Barn, near Bedford, Indiana, was the destination of choice. It provided free accommodations (we slept in a hay loft), shelter from the cold, and it was surrounded by several caves. One of them was Salamander Cave. Salamander Cave was unique because its main passage was the size of a railway tunnel - absolutely huge.

 Salamander Cave was also notorious. Its entrance was low, having to duckwalk through a stream to get into it. After a short distance you could stand up in a water tube and follow it to the main passage, another eighty feet away. Every time it rained the stream inside would swell. In fact, if it rained hard the stream would rise to such an extent that it completely plugged the water tube and entrance, closing off any possibility of escape for those inside. What many people didn't know was that you could easily climb above the rising water in the large chambers, wait awhile for the water to recede, and walk out.

Time after time though, cavers would see the water rising and head for the entrance. Thinking they could make it, they entered the water tube swollen with rushing water, and would tragically drown. I don't know the number, but I do know that the local search and rescue team have visited that cave more times than any other because of that sequence of events.

There I was, young, indestructible, and looking for the next challenge. I learned that there was a small crawlway leaving the water tube near Salamander's entrance that eventually led to a stream and a second entrance about a quarter mile away. A friend and I went to find the exit point of the stream and were a little perplexed upon seeing it. It was a small stream coming out from under a rock in a hill. We were not sure we could get through the hole, so we headed back to Salamander cave and entered the crawlway there.

Now up front let me say that I have done wiser things. About forty feet down the crawlway it came to a dead end, at least we thought it had. With a little exploration we found that we were lying on top of a pile of large rocks that had partially filled in with mud. Fifteen feet below us, we could hear and see the stream flowing. We began to dig and opened a hole large enough to crawl through; almost.

The only way down was headfirst. The hole was so tight I remember actually lifting sections of my stomach and directing them around sharp corners of rock. The last five feet was a drop into the stream bed. After getting ourselves upright again, we saw that we were in a small room. Leading out of the room the stream ran strong. It was about a foot deep and there was another eight inches of air above it. On the bright side, it was nearly ten feet wide.

Down through the stream we went. I led the way. It wasn't long before I realized we had to move slowly through the water. We were laying on our stomachs in the stream, the ceiling being so low we could not lift our heads much, and our mouths were actually submerged in the water. If I held my head sideways, I could breathe but couldn't really see where I was going. To complicate things, whenever I pushed myself forward it would cause a wave. Even with my head turned sideways, the wave would flow by me and cover my mouth.

We experienced a cycle; scoot, hold our breath, hope our open-flamed carbide lamp would not go out, look where we were going, turn our heads, then scoot again. It was laborious and dangerous; a cycle I hope to never repeat.

How many of you are going through that cycle right now? Is your life so splintered that you have to intentionally move, hold your breath, wait for the waves to pass, refocus, and try to move again? I don't know how it is we get to those places in our lives, but each of us has been there, will be there, or is experiencing that cycle right now. Life is pressing so hard that it's difficult to raise your head, get out of bed, and face the day.

Have I told you about my Savior? Have I told you about the *Lifter of Heads*, the *Prince of Peace*, the *Mighty One*? Have I told you of His faithfulness, His love for you, His compassion and mercy? Do you know that no matter where you find yourself today, He knows? He knows you. He knows every pain, every tear, every struggle, every fractured dream, every circumstance, every trial, and every broken heart.

> **"Do you believe that the God of all creation loves and cares about you?"**

Do you believe? Do you believe that the God of all creation loves and cares about you? That He is living and real? That He has counted and ordained the number of hairs on your head and offered his Son Jesus Christ as a sacrifice, to bear your sins on the cross? He is the *Healer of Nations*, the *Ruler of All* and the *Peace Maker*.

God graciously saw us safely out of that little stream passage. We later named it Turtle Cave because that is what you need to be to successfully traverse it. We never attained the other entrance. The ceiling eventually became so low we couldn't continue. But even in that desolate place I learned that God was there. As I reflect back on that time, I realize that it wasn't my strength and initiative that saw me through those underground chambers. Rather it was by the grace of God I saw them, was awed by them and returned safely to those who love me.

Learn a lesson from our experience in Turtle Cave. There is no wave that can overcome you, no darkness that can blind you, or any space that can confine you that will separate you from God's love. He is eternal, He is holy, and He is worthy of all honor and praise.

Matthew 11:28-30 NIV

28"Come to me, all you who are weary and burdened, and I will give you rest. 29Take my yoke upon you and learn from me, for I am gentle and humble in heart, and you will find rest for your souls. 30For my yoke is easy and my burden is light."

A Rich Harvest

God's Bountiful Provision

There is a little town in the heartland of the state of Utah called Mount Pleasant. The name implies a serendipitous opportunity for peace and serenity, yet quite the opposite is true, if you are a turkey. One day in the late fall I was driving to a bank to present some securities investment options to a client. My path took me through Mount Pleasant. As I neared town, the sides of the roads became white. I thought, "Has it snowed here already?" It was mid-November and the air was certainly chilly, yet the day had been clear and enjoyable.

As I closed the distance between me and the town, the white material on either side of the road became deeper, yet I couldn't make out what it was. I stopped the car to investigate and soon found the mounds of white were feathers. Feathers? How could feathers accumulate a foot deep and line the road for miles? I was absolutely amazed and completely confused.

I reentered my car and began following the feathers. Minutes later I came upon a large truck, a flatbed semi stacked to the brim with cages full of white turkeys. As the truck sped down the road, thousands of turkey feathers, being ripped from the hapless birds by the wind, were flying from the cages and settling on both sides of the road. I tailed the big rig for another mile and it turned into the drive of a turkey processing plant.

The light finally came on in my mind. Here, in the middle of nowhere was a thriving industry that raised and processed turkeys, all because of one large company that existed to serve the millions of people who were looking forward to a Thanksgiving dinner. A town that would not exist without Thanksgiving and a way of life directly impacted by how much turkey you eat on Thanksgiving Day. Amazing! So, for our friends in Mount Pleasant, Utah, pig out! Eat turkey until it hurts. Carve the bird, drown your plate with gravy and dribble some on your clothes, there are children depending on you!

Growing up, our family always looked forward to our Thanksgiving experience and meal. My brother recently shared of a time our mother found the Eldorado of turkeys; a 26-pound behemoth that must have strutted and gobbled with a very deep voice. I imagine that before his demise, you would have found this bird pumping iron in the local gym, drinking

"As you thank God for his bountiful provision, consider the most important provision and gift you could ever receive; His Son, nailed to a cross, mocked and scorned for your sake."

protein shakes and shooting steroids. My mother presented it steaming and golden brown on a platter that was way too small, turkey parts hanging off the edge. Eighteen people, family and friends, sat down at the table, each wondering if there would be enough food and who would get the giblets.

Of the 247.6 pounds of grub on the table that day, my favorite was the sweet potatoes; the sweeter the better. Those little golden nuggets dug from the ground have a texture and taste that rivals any food on earth; heavenly. And few places in the world have the bountiful provision that America does. Few meals in the world outpace an American Thanksgiving dinner. Abundance and freedom; things we take for granted yet things that are rare in the rest of the world.

As you thank God for his bountiful provision, consider the most important provision and gift you could ever receive - His Son, nailed to a cross, mocked and scorned for your sake. His purpose was that you might live forever in untenable joy in the glorious presence of your Creator. Perhaps that remembrance of thanks and appreciation will allow you to forgive those who have offended you, those with no excuse. You *can* love them, you *can* forgive them, you *must* forgive them because it is in that same condition you were found when God loved and forgave you; unlovely yet loved; guilty yet forgiven. Praise God for His forgiveness!

Matthew 26:26-28 NIV

[26]While they were eating, Jesus took bread, gave thanks and broke it, and gave it to his disciples, saying, "Take and eat; this is my body." [27]Then he took the cup, gave thanks and offered it to them, saying, "Drink from it, all of you. [28]This is my blood of the[b] covenant, which is poured out for many for the forgiveness of sins.

-Day 24-

Priorities

Abiding in Christ

My wife once asked me after a particularly notorious example of mid-life spending, if I was having a mi-life crisis. I thought about the question and determined in a moment that what I had just purchased was not expensive enough to qualify as a full-blown mid-life crisis acquisition, so I waivered a little and said, "No, not really. I just felt a deep desire for this half inch Makita hammer drill with rotating tension controls, two rechargeable eighteen-volt batteries, and a bonus flashlight."

I believe she was dazzled by the logical and well thought out response because she stood there for a moment with what looked like a slight grimace on her face. In the broad scheme of things, the $249.95 was a drop in the bucket of life, and certainly didn't well represent a momentous occasion like a mid-life crisis!

She went about emptying the kitchen sink of dishes without so much as a word. Occasionally I would hear her talking to herself and my name would come up, but it was hard to hear over the noise of the drill. I was feeling quite proud of dodging her inquiry.

When my battery finally died from constantly running my new toy, the room fell quiet. Anyone who has been married very long knows that periods of quiet after buying an unnecessary tool, while the two of you are alone in the same house, is bad. Accordingly, you could cut the tension with a knife. Carefully and with great self-control she asked, "Was it a mid-life crisis when you bought the new fishing rod last month, or when you bought the wide screen HD TV, or when you bought the motorcycle last week?"

I must admit I was a little taken aback. For a very brief moment I asked myself the same question. I was nearly forty years old. Was I too young for a mid-life crisis? Was I having one? I thought of the American right for all people to bear arms, practice their freedom of religion, and to have a mid-life crisis. No, this can't be a mid-life crisis. That should include buying a Porsche, taking extended vacations, changing careers and the like. No, this couldn't be a mid-life crisis. My response was short and to the point. "No," I said, feeling a little squeamish.

Have you ever had the experience of knowing the words being spoken to you were the source of life or death? Well, my sixth sense picked up on that very quickly. "Then," she responded with clenched teeth, "I will support you even though your recent purchases seem a little out of line." She paused, carefully enunciating every word. "You may have a mid-life crisis, but it better be a good one because you only get one. No more working up to it!" Then the room fell silent once again.

There is a great episode of Home Improvement called *The Look.* Tim Taylor found himself in a similar situation at his friend's hardware store. His wife said more to him through her expression than she did through her words. Suffice it to say, since that moment I carefully weigh every purchase decision against the MLCI (mid-life crisis index) I've developed. After all, I only have one opportunity. And, even though I'm in my mid-sixties, I'm still holding out for the "big one." It seems that using the privilege is a greater potential loss than not using it.

Or perhaps it has just become a dim reality in my life. As I've reflected over the years about the topic, I've come to believe that a mid-life crisis is a self-inflicted condition arising from an improper focus in life, and wrong priorities that shackle our emotions and foresight. It really is an abandoning of what's normal to us. Perhaps it's a dissatisfaction of who we are and what we have. Or an inward focus that demoralizes and compromises our self-worth and rational thinking. Or it's a desire for comfort, pleasure or freedom; I'm not sure.

"If you have received the gift of eternal life through the blood of Jesus, you have been set free, yet we run back to the dungeon wall time after time and lock ourselves up again."

I do know however, that we have an inherent ability to complicate and confuse our lives. If we have received the gift of eternal life through the blood of Jesus, we have been set free, yet we run back to the dungeon wall time after time and lock ourselves up again.

We generate lists of do's and don'ts. We struggle to do this thing right and that thing right, yet we neglect the source of our freedom that as Christians is living in the very heart Christ has given us; the Spirit of the Living God. We spend much of our lives creating laws to abide by, yet we forget to abide *in* Him, the Living Word. That is what I mean by improper focus; the futility of man's institution. The only work that will survive is the work of God. The only one who will survive is the one whose life is captured by the grace and love of Christ.

In a sense, our lives are an enigma. We are free men in Christ, yet we live as prisoners. Everything is possible, yet we limit ourselves. Abiding in Christ is the key that unravels the complexity of life. Being still. Knowing that God loves you. Loving the Wellspring of Life. Communing with the Holy One and understanding that He knows your name. Walking, talking and basking in His mercy and grace: abiding. No need to perform. He will make your paths straight and he will bring peace to your soul. Abide then. Abide in Christ, the Source of all Hope.

Matthew 11:27 NIV

27"All things have been committed to me by my Father. No one knows the Son except the Father, and no one knows the Father except the Son and those to whom the Son chooses to reveal him.

Right Standing
Embracing the Cross

Have you ever stood before a King, or a Queen? Perhaps a president or a governor? If you never have, then it's difficult to understand what it means to reverently fear someone. You see, those offices carry with them the authority to punish and correct our behavior.

Perhaps the closest thing you have experienced is standing before a judge due to a traffic violation or other indiscretion. That judge has a firm grasp on your future; its comfort or discomfort. For most, being in right-standing with an individual who has authority over you is a positive thing, such as when the scriptures instruct children, *obey your parents in the Lord, so that it will go well with you.*

I once was pulled over for not making a full stop at a stoplight. We were in Moab, Utah and a small plane had crashed into an electrical substation, killing all aboard and causing a power outage throughout the town. It was the middle of the night and the town was pitch black. As we drove down Main Street no stop lights were working, nor were any other traffic signals. I glided adeptly through a non-working traffic light which was barely perceptible. What I should have done was to treat the stoplight as a 4-way stop, but it didn't occur to me.

Sitting on a side street was an officer that took exception to my violation and pulled me over. *His* lights were definitely working! Suddenly I found myself in wrong standing with an authority in my life. Not a good place to be. In spite of my reasons, or thinking, I had crossed a line and had to pay the piper. I wish I could say that I took it well, but I didn't. I was incensed that the police officer was insensitive toward me and my situation.

As I have thought back on that encounter, though a rarely used rule, it was a rule none-the-less. If a stoplight is not working, you treat it as a 4-way stop. I think more was at work here as well. God is always in the details, and I had some attitude corrections that needed to be made in my life. This oversight was just the beginning of a deeper growth pattern that God was initiating in me.

I believe one of the difficulties we struggle with is having a true reverence of God. We often find ourselves

> **"I believe one of the difficulties we struggle with is having a true reverence of God"**

"comfortable" with our understanding of things and a Holy God is our second or third thought, not our first. The world creeps into our brains and the reality of who we are in Jesus Christ is foggy. We struggle with reverence for God because we don't prioritize our relationship with him properly. Our eyes are not open to the beauty of the Son.

God, the Eternal Holy One, created you in his image. He provided for your salvation through the blood of his precious son. The cost was high, yet he loved you so much that he made a way; doing for us what we could not do for ourselves.

When Jesus died, God the Father tore the curtain in the temple that separated us from him where he dwelt in the Holy of Holies; from top to bottom. Throughout scripture we read of the grieving process Jewish men went through when they suffered loss. They would grab the top of their robe and tear it (or rend it), ripping it from their chest. It would reveal their heart; the thing that was broken.

God the Father rent the curtain in the temple making a way for us to access Him through Jesus Christ, and I believe in grief for His son. He understood the pain, and sacrifice, and humiliation that Jesus endured for our sakes. If we reject Jesus, there is no sacrifice left, or hope of a righteous future. He has provided a way for us to be in right standing before a Holy God. It is a miracle; that we can be made righteous through Christ.

Please take a moment and think about your relationship with Jesus. Are you in right standing with Him? Have you embraced His gift of life and are you pursuing Him with all your heart? If so, we can say together, "God is very good!" If not, don't delay. Petition Him, seek Him, and He will be found.

There is a day not far away that we will all stand in the presence of God, and we will all kneel before Him confessing that Jesus Christ is Lord; Christian and non-Christian alike. And then we will be separated, the sheep from the goats. May you know the Holy One of Israel as your Lord and Savior. May you have peace.

Romans 14:10-12 NIV

10 You, then, why do you judge your brother or sister? Or why do you treat them with contempt? For we will all stand before God's judgment seat. 11 It is written: "'As surely as I live,' says the Lord, 'every knee will bow before me; every tongue will acknowledge God.'" 12 So then, each of us will give an account of ourselves to God.

Sojourn

The Eyes of God

Articulated fingers of cirrus clouds licked the underside of the huge wings supporting our plane as we began our final approach to the island. It pensively awaited our arrival reaching up with craggy mountain peaks as if to ward off the impending collision between the wheels of our plane and the earth. The heavily forested island appeared as a distorted green dot set below us in a sea of blue water. Peering out the window, we could see breakers near the shore as our plane tipped its wings for the last time before drifting gently onto the runway.

The reverse thrusters threw us forward in our seats and the plane slowed to a taxi eventually parking on the tarmac. We had been planning our trip to the Dominican Republic for quite some time and were anxious to see the island. After a long, slow process involving multiple protocols, we stepped out of the plane, down the steps and onto the ground. The air was heavy with humidity and the heat stifling; at least ninety degrees. We secured our luggage at the back of the craft and were ushered into a small area detached from the main terminal to be processed through customs.

The scene reminded me of Casablanca; men in sweaty stained uniforms, overhead fans turning almost imperceptibly, dark red letters headlining the entrance in Spanish communicating the purpose of the building, and large palm trees all around.

Long lines formed at the three stations as officials scrutinized every individual seeking entry into their country. One lady even had all of her belongings spread across a table as a uniformed man groped through what remained in her luggage looking for contraband.

"Good grief," I thought. I don't want my things ravaged!" I stepped forward and handed the official my passport, he looked at me and asked, "Sir, why do you visit Republica de Dominicana?"

"I'm here for a one-week vacation," I said. "I've always wanted to visit." His face broke into a wide smile revealing years of oral neglect. Many of his teeth were missing, and those still present needed serious dental attention.

"Welcome to our country," he said handing me my passport. "You may go."

Several of our group, including my wife Becky, gathered our things and stepped out onto the sidewalk paralleling the building. The heat seemed to settle on us like a heavy soup collecting as droplets of perspiration. Some relief came as a gentle breeze tickled the drops forming on my forehead. I wiped them off with my handkerchief, also drying the headband of my hat.

A busy city scene unfolded in front of us. People were everywhere. Trucks and busses were almost as numerous as the motorcycles and bicycles. Armed policemen were on nearly every corner wielding machine guns, and the occasional shotgun, both demanding respect in an otherwise chaotic environment. The busses we had chartered were waiting with their engines running ready to receive our large group. Our destination was two and a half hours away, sitting on the southeast side of the island: *Casa de Campo.*

The average income per capita in the Dominican Republic was under $300 per year. This meant that most people ate lizards, and whatever else they could scavenge, along with the occasional chicken. We traveled for two hours through the countryside and pulled into Casa de Campo, one of the most beautiful places I have ever been. The resort consisted of several hundred acres set directly on the ocean. A steward escorted us each to our rooms. They were located in bungalows set throughout the grounds, each containing four rooms.

What we noticed immediately was the contrast between the real Dominican Republic and the place we were staying. At the time, the cost of our rooms was more per night than the average annual income of the general population. Management of the operation was easy. One inconsistency or one doubt and you were fired - no questions asked. There were a thousand more people vying for the same position ready to work at a moment's notice.

Many who visited felt uncomfortable and out-of-place knowing that our lives where lived in opulence, if even for a short time, through the labor of the deeply impoverished. People struggled for existence. In the midst of all the beauty a real sense of hopelessness existed. We could see it in the eyes of the people begging us for help and hoping for a brighter future.

I realized that we are the few that own more than we can carry on our backs. I realized that God has blessed us with much and will require much from us. Becky and I felt in many ways ashamed; ashamed at the glut of wealth we had and our cluelessness to the DR people's condition. We wanted to leave everything we had brought with us, and to ship back much more when we returned home. I wonder how many might have been saved through a concerted effort of a few people helping. I wonder how many might have heard the Gospel or had full bellies?

We take so many things for granted in this country and we cry foul when things don't go according to our plans, yet we can't see the suffering of those around us. We struggle to see even our own condition. I pray that God would do a good work in us. That He might do for us what He did for Paul; open the eyes of our heart that we might see clearly.

I do pray that God would open the eyes of your heart, that He would enable you to see the beauty and value of what he has done for you, and that He would help you see the immense value of others. You see, everything we have is a gift from God; a provision of His love. Take a moment to examine your heart. Ask God to show you any inconsistencies and then ask Him to open your eyes to His purpose and plan for your life. His word is sharper than any double-edged sword. It penetrates even to dividing soul and spirit, joints and marrow, and He is faithful to save us from our sin.

"I do pray that God would open the eyes of your heart, that He would enable you to see the beauty and value of what He has done for you, and that He would help you see the immense value of others."

Ephesians 1:15-19 NIV

[15]For this reason, ever since I heard about your faith in the Lord Jesus and your love for all the saints, [16]I have not stopped giving thanks for you, remembering you in my prayers. [17]I keep asking that the God of our Lord Jesus Christ, the glorious Father, may give you the Spirit of wisdom and revelation, so that you may know him better. [18]I pray also that the eyes of your heart may be enlightened in order that you may know the hope to which he has called you, the riches of his glorious inheritance in the saints, [19]and his incomparably great power for us who believe.

-Day 27-

Family

Love that Makes a Difference

As I grew up, I had three sets of grandparents. My mother's mother was remarried, as was her father. It's interesting as an adult to look back at how they impacted my life. For example, my grandma Dare was always encouraging, nurturing and oozy-sweet to me. My grandma Blech was matter of fact, somewhat demanding (always asking us to clean up our messes), yet her love for us was very evident. My grandma Ethel was not very warm and fuzzy either. Living in California, we saw her infrequently yet always enjoyed our times together.

My grandpa Blech was a jovial, light-hearted individual who loved to show off his pipe collection while Grandpa Dare was a case. He was a "gentleman" chicken farmer with a short fuse that often ignited over seemingly insignificant occurrences. Grandpa Smith was a clothier who was very generous. Each time we visited he would have us pick out clothes from his store, providing a new outfit for the coming school year.

Times at grandma and Grandpa Dare's chicken farm were joyous for me. I looked forward to spending several days with them each summer as I grew up. They lived near Walkerton, Indiana which was not too far from Koontz Lake; a favorite fishing and swimming hole. My parents would pack me up and drive the half-hour to their place, frequently stopping at the general store in a nearby town to buy a sweet treat.

The total property was about five acres and had a small section of woods in the back. It was elongated with two huge chicken coops sitting parallel to its length. The house structure connected the two coops and the lower level served as a shop and grain storage area. It also held the only bathroom in the building. Up a set of rickety stairs was the living area. The door opened into the kitchen which flowed into a small living room and two bedrooms.

Grandpa Dare raised Irish Setters, a beautiful breed of hunting dog with long red hair. They were penned behind the house in an enclosure that contained their enthusiasm for visitors. Upon arrival I'd often run out to the pens to greet the active dogs. Some were sweet-as-can-be, others would bark and even growl at me, but I took it all in stride. I'd then run up the stairs to receive a waiting hug from my grandma, and occasionally would receive one from grandpa too. Then it was straight to the back bedroom where I knew I'd sleep. Without fail, when I entered that room there was a pile of comic books on the bed, lovingly placed there by Grandma. Donald Duck, Scrooge McDuck, The Green Hornet, Superman, and many other wonderful comic book characters drew my imagination into their world.

The feeling of love from Grandma and the total lack of responsibility during my stays were major draws for me. Rising early and heading to the woods for a morning of play under the fallen trees was an activity that raised both excitement and a sense of adventure in me. And every time I'd had enough and dragged myself, exhausted from playing, back to grandma's house, there she would be waiting to serve me a plate of cookies, or a sandwich, or a bowl of hot soup. She treated me as if I were the only reason she awoke that day; to make sure my day was special.

My times at Grandma Blech's house were always filled with work, yet in many ways it was satisfying. One of Grandma's frequent fall activities was to harvest and shell black walnuts. I remember at her funeral recalling the uncommon activity. She would go to her basement where there were bushels of walnuts straight from the tree. She would then solicit my help to begin shucking their greenish/black skin from around the actual nut. What I remember above all else is that every time we shucked black walnuts; our hands turned the same color: black. They would stay black for many weeks. But oh, the sweet candy she made with them. She would turn those nuts into scrumptious divinity, a sticky, sugary delight that is still a favorite of mine. And she did it with love; with a desire to please the ones she was creating them for.

I seemed to bond closest to my two grandmothers in Indiana. Though significantly different in character and action, they had a common theme in their lives; they desired to love and honor their families. From Grandma Dare I learned to love even when that action was difficult, serving others even if it meant sacrifice on my part, and to respect people for who they are. From Grandma Blech I learned to be practical, to watch out for those you love, and to be frugal. I learned a little hard work wouldn't hurt me and that it actually made me feel better even though I was often sore and tired. And now I am a little bit like her having observed her tenacious spirit and unwavering will.

I wish they had each written a book that shared more of their lives so that I could glean from the wisdom they had **"Why is it we keep learning those lessons over and over, generation after generation, when so many that have gone before us have already learned lessons that could smooth our path in life?"** accumulated over their long lives. Why is it we keep learning those lessons over and over, generation after generation, when so many that have gone before us have already learned lessons that could smooth our path in life? All we have to do is view and reflect on the lives of others; to be life-long learners. Our lack of learning often results in pain and suffering in our own lives.

And I think of the tremendous love our Father has for us in the person of Jesus Christ. Of the detailed instruction He left us through the Bible to secure our futures, and I ask the same question. Jesus, like my grandparents, has sacrificially loved us yet to a much greater extent. The stakes are much higher and the outcomes more important. If you love Him and abide in Him, little by little you become more like Him. He has promised to seal His Word in your heart and to transform you into His very image. Like growing up in Indiana and being part of the lives of my grandparents, Christ has provided for us a family; the perfect family. In Him we are grafted into *His* family; the family of God. And with this comes a great inheritance and a compelling outcome; we are His forever.

Father, rapture my heart and indelibly burn the name of my Savior Jesus into my soul that I may never look to myself or the world again for my fulfillment, comfort or significance. Tightly hold my life so that the imprint of your arms and the words of your mouth will forever remain a part of who I am - my very essence.

Colossians 1:15-18 NIV

[15]He is the image of the invisible God, the firstborn over all creation. [16]For by him all things were created: things in heaven and on earth, visible and invisible, whether thrones or powers or rulers or authorities; all things were created by him and for him. [17]He is before all things, and in him all things hold together. [18]And he is the head of the body, the church; he is the beginning and the firstborn from among the dead, so that in everything he might have the supremacy.

-Day 28-

Reflection

Our Identity in Christ

Reflection, like seeing your image in a pool, reveals much; the shape of your face, or your torso, or stature. The sky may be revealed behind you, and the nuances of your form. As long as the water in the pool is still, the reflection is perfect. Yet throw a rock in the pool and waves will begin to ripple out from the center, distorting the image you see.

As we consider our Christian lives, the enemy is constantly throwing rocks in our pool, trying to mask who we are in Christ. He is an identity stealer; a distorter of truth. He seeks to place a wedge between us and God, siphoning hope from our souls. Yet, God is faithful. He has already defeated our enemy. He will always listen and respond to us. We are simply called to believe what he says and to fix our eyes on Jesus.

There is nothing more freeing than to converse with God about the struggles and victories of your life. "Father, I really, really blew it with my spouse today. Father, I am so sad I think my heart will break. Father, I don't know why I lied, there was no point. Father, forgive me for the way I spoke to her, help me to see her as you do."

Each of us is faced with unique challenges and situations in our lives. We are moved by deep emotions we can't explain. We are torn by sinful patterns we can't control. We are longing for something better; for peace and quiet. We struggle with knowing the answer to life's most difficult questions. "Why did we lose such a special person? Why can't I pay my bills? Why is it so hard to talk to him? When will my struggles ever end?"

Where is it you go to talk to God? What place do you identify as your special place where you meet God face to face and pour your heart out? My dear wife has been very supportive of my adventures. One of the reasons she is supportive is that she knows me very well. Apart from God, she knows me better than anyone on this planet; and she knows that I have a deep-seated need to commune with God in the wilderness. That is my special place. A place where I can leave the busyness of life behind and talk unencumbered with my Father.

It often looks like this, "Honey, I need to get away for a few days. Will that be OK?" She hears this every year or so and knows immediately what I'm up to. She knows it's time for me to head to some remote woods or mountain and walk and talk with the love of my life, Jesus. No jealously. No hard feelings. No second thoughts just *yes,* every time sending me with her blessing to meet with my God. And what special times those are.

One such outing took me to the Cascade Mountains in Oregon which are tropical in character and nestled closely to the Pacific Ocean. The undergrowth in the Cascades is so thick that's it's nearly impossible to hike cross-country. Established trails and roads are the best way to move through the terrain. I had a general area in mind and was excited about the outing.

Soon I was in our Buick, the trunk loaded with camping gear, looking for a remote location. I headed up a dirt road, common in the region because of the extensive logging that takes place there and began scouting numerous sites. I came across a dry creek bed about 2 miles up the road and stopped in the middle of it.

The creek bed was wide and meandered off into the wilderness, disappearing around a corner about a thousand feet away. The base of the creek bed was like a cobblestone street; relatively smooth yet bumpy. I made the decision to turn into the bed and head up the cobblestone. The going was slow because I didn't want to tear the muffler off, but the route was passable. Soon the trees closed in on both sides and the creek bed narrowed. The walls of the path raised on either side until, if you were an observer, you would only have seen the top of my car from ground level.

As I continued, I thought how ridiculous I must look, driving up a creek in the middle of nowhere - in a Buick! No roads in sight, deer staring at me like I was an alien in his spacecraft, and small animals of all kinds running in fear of their lives. And then the thought struck me: "What if I break down out here?" No one would ever find me.

Persisting, I came across another dirt road that intersected the stream and quickly took my exit, thankful for a second opportunity. The road led me to a small lake, void of people and absolutely beautiful. I found a quiet spot in the hemlock trees that lined it and set up camp. The next two days were special beyond words; no interruptions and no agendas. It was just me in my torn jeans and God my Father ministering to me through his unexplainable mercy and grace.

We covered a lot of ground that day. I sought and clearly received the forgiveness and fellowship of the One who is pure love. Gentle breezes, sunny clearings, the strong smell of balsam and the refreshing Water of Life. And I knew when it was time to go. My thoughts turned to my wife and family and I packed in haste, with great anticipation of being reunited. Then and now, my family is the greatest gift God has given me, only being trumped by Christ himself.

Those times made me consider how it must have been as God walked with Adam in the garden. No agendas, no deadlines and no expectations. Just pure communion and **"And as you walk with God in sweet fellowship, the reflection of who you are as a man becomes very clear."** connecting with God in a way that encourages and that strengthens. And as you walk with God in sweet fellowship, the reflection of who you are as a man becomes very clear. You are His. You are cherished. You are grafted into the family of God, a child of the King; royalty. It's a pure reflection that can be hard to see, yet through the blood of Christ, though riddled with sin and shortcomings, you are made perfect.

The next time you look into a mirror, ask God to reflect back into your eyes the true person you are - a joy to behold!

1 Corinthians 13:8-13 NIV

[8]Love never fails. But where there are prophecies, they will cease; where there are tongues, they will be stilled; where there is knowledge, it will pass away. [9]For we know in part and we prophesy in part, [10]but when perfection comes, the imperfect disappears. [11]When I was a child, I talked like a child, I thought like a child, I reasoned like a child. When I became a man, I put childish ways behind me. [12]Now we see but a poor reflection as in a mirror; then we shall see face to face. Now I know in part; then I shall know fully, even as I am fully known. [13]And now these three remain: faith, hope and love. But the greatest of these is love.

An Epiphany
Trusting God

Somewhere between the age of 18 and 60, I had an epiphany. I came to the realization that I was destructible, and that pain really did hurt. If you focus on some of the recreational activities I've engaged in, especially when a teenager, you would think I had no understanding of that fact. Jumping off of a 300-foot cliff on an 11mm rope? Dubious. Doing it as fast as I could? Questionable. Doing it upside down to see what it felt like? Well, you understand.

And those other things I loved to do like heading to a remote wilderness place with no food to see how long I could make it. My personal best was five days, but I didn't starve. I ate grouse, squirrel, fish, rose hips, and cattails. I was a regular Daniel Boone.

I think I had a glimmer of my epiphany when I was 18 years old and crawling through another cave in southern Indiana. I came carelessly flying out of a very muddy passage about fifteen feet above a stream. On the way down I caught and broke my ankle on a sharp, protruding rock. We were nearly a mile back in the cave and yes, it was painful. I quickly shook off the warning however, pulled out two flashlights, used them to splint my ankle and crawled out of the cave on my rear. Just a little "bump in life," I thought. I was so covered in mud that the hospital I was taken to had to cut the clothes off of me and completely clean the room I occupied.

I share that to confirm that life's lessons are often learned the hard way. It seems too often that no amount of counsel, warning or pleading will shift us from our path when we are heading the way we want to go. Yet God, in His infinite wisdom understands that and allows some difficult; and yes, even painful experiences to enter our lives. He knows that true change can only be accomplished by Him; the transformation of our hearts being the end goal. As we live through those experiences, we each become very proficient at prayer. What is so amazing is that God is absolutely faithful and trustworthy as He walks with us through those trials.

I am not suggesting that every trial we endure is a result of our straying. I am saying, however, that whatever trial we endure will change us, like clay being sculpted by the Master Potter. Take for example, the events of July 2001.

The air was a warm 65 degrees when I awoke in the early morning to head for the Uinta Mountains in northeastern Utah. The weather was clear and promising. It took only thirty minutes to load my friend Todd and my nephew Ben into the SUV. We pulled through an all-night McDonalds at 4:00 a.m. and began the three-hour drive to our trailhead. The sun was rising rapidly, and the air was chilled as we reached the 11,200-foot trailhead at the end of a long dirt road. No signs, no welcomes, just the end of the road and a looming mountain ahead of us. Ben and I strapped on our backpacks and said goodbye to Todd who would meet us again in 6 days on the Mirror Lake highway, some 65 miles away from our present location.

We waved goodbye and began to hike the beautiful country ahead. The day was forecast to have a high of 75 degrees down in Salt Lake City so we knew it would be amazing in the mountains. So sure was I of the route ahead that I had considered leaving my rain gear to save weight, yet a little voice told me to hang onto those outer garments.

Ben was visiting from northern Indiana and joined me on the hike. He loves the outdoors and was excited about the trip. The country was breath-taking. It seemed every step revealed a new, awe-inspiring view or feature of the wilderness we were hiking through. The elevation varied from 11,000 feet to as high as 13,500 feet (Kings Peak). The section we were traveling that morning fluctuated very little and was a pleasure to walk. Beautiful lakes and rumbling streams greeted us over and over again as we reveled in God's creation.

It wasn't until mid-afternoon that we realized something was wrong. The chilly mountain air became even colder. We were only wearing medium weight sweaters, but the air became so cold we had to pull out our rain gear and put it on. I kept rationalizing that this was the middle of July and the forecast was for clear weather. The chill must be temporary. In the late afternoon it began to snow, first a little, then very hard, then horizontally with 25-30 mile per hour winds! Wait a minute. Wait just a minute! This is July!

I was stunned. Our hands became colder and colder, and it was difficult to see each other as the storm intensified. Our core body temperature must have dropped because we both began to shiver. I knew that if we didn't find shelter quickly, the ferocious wind would sap every ounce of heat from our bodies. Once again, I became a really, really good pray-er.

 We dropped down off of the ridge we'd been walking into a broad and gently sloping valley. It was treeless as far as we could see, and the wind continued to drive against us. Out of the now darkening, snowy landscape we made out a small clump of trees and in a few steps, we were in them. The area consisted of three weather beaten subalpine fir trees. Though the area was small, the trees were large enough that we were able to stand behind them and get some relief from the wind.

There was no possibility of a fire. The only way to survive the night was to get into our tents and into our sleeping bags where we would be away from the wind, and warm. Food didn't matter, water really didn't matter, just warmth. Ben was carrying a small one-man tent which he fought to set up in the gale. I on the other hand, was carrying nothing but a hammock; a Hennessey Hammock. These hammocks are constructed from very light material, having a full mesh covering to protect you from bugs and a rain fly to keep out the rain. However, they are not designed to endure a snowstorm.

I hung the hammock between two of the trees and crawled into a sleeping bag rated to 20 degrees. All night the wind howled, and the hammock rocked back and forth. I frequently asked Ben if he was OK and to my surprise, he always responded in the affirmative. Tough kid! By morning the wind had stopped. As I dropped out of the hammock, I landed in nearly two feet of fresh, glistening snow. It was beautiful and surreal! I felt like an Eskimo digging out of a hole in the frozen north.

> **"Either I would trust God to see me through the difficulty I found myself in, or I would not."**

During the night, I had a lot of time to think - I certainly didn't sleep! I felt the weight of responsibility for my nephew and wondered how we would hike out in the snow. I wondered if we would even see the morning and considered my family. I also thought about my life and realized that this was the storm the disciples faced in their boat. This was the fear Gideon felt as he approached a hopeless situation. This was the torrent crashing around Noah's Ark. I needed to make a decision that night. Either I would trust God to see us through the difficulty we found ourselves in, or I would not.

Like committing to a marriage, or raising children, or investing your life into someone, love is a decision; a choice. Our world and our media correlates love with a feeling, a sense of nirvana, but it's not. Love is not an emotion, but it is emotional. It is really a commitment and illumination to the value of the one you love, and a surrender of self. I loved Ben and was willing to do whatever it took to see him safely home. I knew that trusting God in our circumstance was the path to accomplish that.

We trudged through miles of deep snow. Seemly impossible obstacles were overcome every mile as we made our way off of the mountain. We had to hike a long, long way to get to a place we could be picked up for a ride home. Blisters welted our feet causing discomfort and pain, yet we continued to walk with focused thoughts in our minds; a hot meal, a warm house, and the love of our family. As I reflect on that time and the conditions we encountered, it was only God that could have seen us through. Only He could have brought about the series of events necessary to see us to safety.

Where is it you draw strength from? Who is it you trust in? Loving God begins with trust; a trust that you are valuable to Him, a trust that He will walk with you through whatever you may encounter, and a trust that he knows your name. Our God is absolutely faithful to do more than you can imagine. You will never be disappointed in trusting Him. You will never be ashamed of the cross. For the Lamb sacrificed that day is the Wellspring of Life, the Hope of Nations and the source of our joy. No matter where you find yourself today, I encourage you to lean on the Cornerstone, the Rock of our Salvation.

Psalm 95:1-2 NIV

[1] Come, let us sing for joy to the LORD; let us shout aloud to the Rock of our salvation. [2] Let us come before him with thanksgiving and extol him with music and song.

You are not Alone

Christmas at Grandma's

The house was filled with joy as we entered my grandmother's home in Northern Indiana. Waves of comforting heat danced on our cheeks from the fire she had built up in her fireplace. The blast of warmth defrosted our fingers and faces which had been chilled by the -15°F air that attacked us between the car and the front door. Grandma Blech was a widow, though I really didn't understand what that meant, and lived in a humble home; small yet well-kept and inviting.

In the living room she had set up multiple tables pressed together to seat our large family for Christmas dinner. They were lovingly covered with festive adornments fitting the season. The house smelled fabulous with hints of ham and pie filling the air and on the fireplace mantle sat five of those pies, each assembled with the love and care grandma was known for. The star was her Christmas pie which was piled high with sweet meringue. It looked like layers of clouds inviting you into the folds of its delectable goodness. It always had a flaky crust and was sprinkled with colorful fruits in its custard base. I am longing for it even now. What an amazing desert!

Grandma was no nonsense, always telling it the way it was from her perspective, yet in love. "Comb your hair!" "Eat your vegetables!" and "Don't you sass your mom!" were typical phrases we heard. As we walked in, she barked, "Wipe your feet!" then gave each of us a bear hug and a kiss. You see, she truly loved us, pouring herself into each of our lives as we grew up during a restless time in history. We piled the presents we were carrying for her under the white pine Christmas tree she had decorated for the season. The presents fell into a great pile mingling with the meticulously wrapped gifts she had prepared for each of us.

One thing that always blessed me about Grandma Blech was that she knew us, each and every one. Yes, she knew our names, but she also knew our likes and dislikes, our dreams and passions, and our foibles; and she loved us anyway. She knew us because she took the time to get to know us. We weren't just her daughter's children, we were special, loved and cherished just as we were. What an amazing feeling wells up in me even today, many years after her passing, knowing that I was loved by her. Just speaking her name brings back a flood of wonderful memories. Grandma Blech.

What happens in your heart when you speak the name of Jesus Christ? Is there peace, joy and thankfulness? Are there wonderful memories?

"What happens in your heart when you speak the name of Jesus Christ?"

Not only does He know your name, but He also knows your heart, your needs, your fears, and your dreams. He is the Giver of Life and the Restorer of all that is broken. He knitted you together in your mother's womb and breathed life into your body, and He has secured your future for eternity through His death and resurrection. And did you know that he loves you beyond measure?

When we met as a family, grandma would always sit us down to a feast, a feast prepared with her loving hands. The fellowship, the food and the conversation surrounding the meal brought joy to our hearts and peace to our lives. Those meals were special because the one who invited us was special.

Dear friends, a day is coming in the near future when the love of our life, Jesus Christ, will sit us down to a banquet. It will be a time of joy, of fellowship and of delight. The blessings we will receive will have just begun because the Host, the Bridegroom, loves us and has prepared a place for us in heaven. He is the hope for mankind. He is our Savior. I pray you will experience peace, joy, family, and hope as you squarely place your faith in the Prince of Peace, Jesus Christ.

John 14:1-4 NIV

[1]"Do not let your hearts be troubled. You believe in God; believe also in me. [2]My Father's house has many rooms; if that were not so, would I have told you that I am going there to prepare a place for you? [3]And if I go and prepare a place for you, I will come back and take you to be with me that you also may be where I am. [4]You know the way to the place where I am going."

-Day 31-

Coyote Rodeo!

How will you be Remembered?

The sun rose begrudgingly over the frozen landscape. Every branch, every tree and every blade of grass was encased in a layer of ice that pulled it toward the ground like a cowboy throwing a roped steer. The burden carried had already broken off limbs and threatened to take down whole blocks of forest. For the past twenty-four hours snow and sleet had collected on the unwilling recipients changing the countryside into a stark, frosty scene.

The ice had so transformed the landscape it seemed as if we stepped off of Admiral Byrd's Norwegian ship the *City of New York*, onto the continent of Antarctic, except there were no dog sleds waiting. The ice had formed a crunchy layer over the 5-feet of snow that had accumulated over the winter.

Three of us, fancying ourselves mountain men of sorts, had planned a backpacking trip into the mountains above Logan, Utah. We thought backpacking in winter on snowshoes would be high adventure yet were surprised by the conditions that faced us as we stepped out of the truck. We had expected some snow, but the ice was an unwanted obstacle. The resulting landscape proved to be a slippery challenge to our otherwise well-planned outing.

Our destination was Old Ephraim's grave, high up a canyon intersecting a road spur off highway 89, east of the town. Old Ephraim was the monarch of the mountain, and the last known grizzly bear to inhabit the Wasatch range. He stood 9-feet 11-inches on his hind legs and weighed nearly 1,100 pounds. Old Ephraim led a sordid life; harassing ranchers, eating sheep and cattle, and generally being a nuisance. His escapades continued until a rancher being impacted had enough. The rancher managed to trap the beast and bring him to terms, ending the life of a legend.

As we attacked the trail, ice and snow clung to our shoes adding unwanted weight and exertion to our efforts. Tenacious little branches of brush sticking above the surface of the snow reached out for our snowshoes, often tripping us. It was as if they were warning us to go no further, unsuccessfully trying to halt our course forward.

Several times this resulted in one of us upside-down in a drift and unable to get up. On our backs in the snow, the packs became like anchors pulling us deeper into the drifts. When we tried to push against the snow to right ourselves, it offered no foundation and we just flailed in the hole we had created. Only after a helping hand was offered were we able to stand erect again.

We headed up the canyon seeking a site to camp for the night. That's a difficult task when you're walking on top of deep snow. The hike was only six miles; yet for every step we took, it seemed like ten. We carried thirty-five pounds of gear each, were headed uphill and waddled like ducks atop our bear-paw shaped snowshoes.

We had learned through survival books that the snow depth is less under trees that sit near the bottom of steep slopes. We found such a place and began to dig out a site for our camp. Down we dug, approximately four feet, leaving a square hole just big enough to fit the three of us lying down. We had a small tarp that was big enough to cover two thirds of the hole (and consequently two people) and I was the odd guy out. For me, the stars were amazing, so I had no qualms about sleeping under them, even in the winter

We lined the bottom of the hole with pine boughs to insulate us from the cold, laid down a sleeping pad and stretched out our goose down sleeping bags. We felt pretty smug about the place we had labored to build - it should be a good night.

Settling in, we pulled the strings on our mummy bags, knowing we would be warm and comfortable. We also laid the armory we'd brought with us next to our bags...just in case. My friends each carried a .22 rifle and I carried a 20-gauge shotgun. There is a certain assurance that comes with having a shotgun lying next to you in the middle of the wilderness. In the still of the darkness my two companions dozed off and were soon releasing visible wisps of moisture from the breathing holes formed in the hoods of their bags.

As I lay there trying to identify stars, coyotes began to yelp, first quietly in the distance, then closer, and closer. They raised a chorus that echoed throughout the valley. It was clear there was a pack of the canines chasing something down the narrow canyon we were sleeping in. The ruckus awoke my friends as the noise of the pack intensified. The coyotes were so close that we were immediately on full alert.

We truly thought the animals, intent on pursuing some poor mountain critter, would accidentally jump right into our bedroom. From the surface, you could barely tell the hole we were sleeping in was there, except for the tarp strung over one end. Certainly, in the dark they would have no warning of the impending collision. I imagined what it would be like to wrestle with a coyote, snarling and snapping its teeth at me, while I was forcibly trying to eject it from our hole.

Then the musky smell of dog entered our nostrils as the coyotes came directly at us. Click! Click! Click! Three rounds were chambered in our firearms, the noise shattering the cold, still air. We all raised the weapons we had brought in anticipation of the assault, praying there were no more than three animals to attend to.

"Don't shoot me," I whispered as we heard the imaginary order to set bayonets and prepare for close-quarters combat. At that moment, the coyotes were upon us, snarling and confused by the obstacle in front of them. They were a pack of five animals, and it turned out they were chasing a mule deer. The deer veered to the side of our abode, kicking snow on top of me. The coyotes responded in chase like a slow-motion scene out of

White Fang; tongues flailing, slobber flying, eyes and soul intent on the prey they were about to capture.

Our adrenaline was running strong as I thought about the need of those animals to secure a meal, and then about the deer and its desire to be free of the menace trying to end its life. I thought of the epic struggle for survival all creation goes through daily. I pondered the need for food and the loss surrounding death, then all grew quiet again. The pack had moved further down the canyon until we could barely hear the sounds of the chase.

The next morning, we arose early, made some camp coffee, and gathered our snowshoes, curious about how the chase had ended. We hiked about a half-mile down the canyon in the direction we'd entered following the tracks of the pack. And then we saw it, a bloody stained section of snow and only pieces of the deer left scattered around, barely identifying the animal that had passed our way the night before. The coyotes won...the deer lost. Five coyotes had full, happy stomachs, and possibly the deer would be missed. I actually contemplated that for a while and my thoughts turned to my life. How will I be remembered? Have I loved those people God has brought into my life?

Standing there in the snow, taking in the scene, I began to talk to God. I turned and headed up the canyon to break camp, and I remember my mood was sober. I asked God the same question I had asked myself, "Have I loved those you've put in my life?"

I believe that was a pivotal time for me. I was young, fearless and, at times, very difficult to be around. I was proud and self-focused, yet God knew who I was then, and He knew who I would become. I had no idea the path of life He had put me on in order to change me into a man that reflects Him. I have no idea the path He will chart for me between today and the day I enter His presence. But I know one thing; I was created to love Him.

"But I know one thing; I was created to love Him."

When you are gone and your life on earth is over, how will you be remembered? Will your loss be mourned? Will your works withstand the Refiner's fire? Love the Lord your God with all your heart, soul, and mind, and love those He has put in your life…for God is love. May you be a living testament of the Savior.

1 John 4:7-12 NIV

[7]Dear friends, let us love one another, for love comes from God. Everyone who loves has been born of God and knows God. [8]Whoever does not love does not know God, because God is love. [9]This is how God showed his love among us: He sent his one and only Son[b] into the world that we might live through him. [10]This is love: not that we loved God, but that he loved us and sent his Son as an atoning sacrifice for[c] our sins. [11]Dear friends, since God so loved us, we also ought to love one another. [12]No one has ever seen God; but if we love one another, God lives in us and his love is made complete in us.

River Watchers

The Line Between Heaven and Earth

Are you a river watcher? I mean, have you spent time watching water slip down a cool stream, bubble over rocks, dip into holes, and spray into the sky when it hits an obstruction? I have. I've experienced the roar of a stream rushing down a steep incline and the coolness of deep pools under the branches of old tortured trees.

Standing near a river, or following its path, brings peace and stirs the soul. And as you engage in the sights before you, the noise of rushing water blocks out most other sounds and intrusions. You are able to relax, focus and dream of days gone by.

In the eddy of a river where the fast water meets the slack water, currents turn back upriver, obeying the forces that compel them and forming a shifting line. On one side of the line the water is moving so quickly downriver that few things escape its grasp, yet on the other side, the water moves slowly in the opposite direction. As you approach the line between the two currents, constant change and fluctuation is taking place. Water molecules in one moment are headed full bore down their path, only to be sucked into the slow water and be carried back upstream. Though the two currents slip past each other, comingling at times, the actual line of separation between the two is indistinct and blurred.

If you enjoy fishing, that line is a great place to drop a bobber. Fish love to hang out in the slower current and pursue likely meals that slip by. The line between the fast and slow water also tends to hold your bobber in a slow march up and down the eddy, giving you lots of time for a potential bite. Many a wily fisherman has pulled praise-worthy catches from such places.

Isn't that how our walk should be as Christians? We should be so engaged in both sides of the line that the distinction between the two is blurred. We walk in the world which takes us like a rushing stream down a defined course. Yet we hit that edge, that edge of heavenly engagement, and are pulled to the slack water for renewal, rest and encouragement. We walk in the world, yet our eyes are set on Jesus, our Hope. We walk, we talk, we adore, we read, we live in relationship, we pray, and we bolster our faith in the strength of God. Those are the eddies of our lives; the quiet moments of communion with God.

When we walk in this way, not only is our future glorious beyond description, but our day to day life has victory. We make a difference. We bring light to darkness and hope to the hopeless. We participate in

"Be so engaged with Jesus and heavenly purposes that the line between heaven and earth is blurred, not sure whether you're standing in heaven or on earth."

miracles and walk with God on this earth. We are ambassadors of Christ.

Be a river watcher. Live in the line between the fast and slack water. Be so engaged with Jesus and heavenly purposes that the line between heaven and earth is blurred, not sure whether you're standing in heaven or on earth. You are a holy people, a royal priesthood, a people set apart by God. Don't merely exist, but exist for Him; the King of Kings, the Prince of Peace.

Revelation 5:12

12Worthy is the Lamb, who was slain, to receive power and wealth and wisdom and strength and honor and glory and praise!

Deep calls to deep in the roar of your waterfalls. Psalm

Epilogue
A Note from the Author

One of the things I love about writing, is seeing my children engage in the concepts and activities of authoring their own devotions. This is a devotion, with artwork, that my daughter Pauline penned. The lesson is profound and the delivery engaging. Please enjoy these words of encouragement. *S R Dare*

My Philodendron
Thirsting for God ~ by Pauline Cox

In my kitchen I have a philodendron that has been part of my life for the past 10 years. I bought it to add a little light and life to my first classroom. It began a mere six inches long, with two small shoots and a smattering of vibrant variegated leaves.

That first year it lived in its original pot off the left-behind water bottles of my sixth-grade students. It was a new start, a fresh beginning. Over time, my sweet little vine began to grow and change. It soon outgrew its original home and needed a place to stretch and grow.

It has moved with me to three states and currently resides on top of my kitchen cabinets. It has grown well over six feet long, and I often have to trim it to keep it from overtaking my entire kitchen. In its current home, I still enjoy its beauty and notice its growth, but far less frequently than when it first sat in the windowsill by my school desk.

Normally, it's as it began; bright, cheerful, leaves lifted high and stretching for the sun beams shining through the window. However, there are other times when life gets busy, and I forget my sweet, leafy friend. I am ashamed to admit I will busily go about my daily life and never once look up, sometimes for as many as four weeks at a time. Then one day, I pause, and notice how my philodendron's leaves have yellowed, and others are drooping. It is still hanging on, but only just.

What it needs is for me to climb on a chair and fill its pot with water. Within hours of doing this, every leaf is once again full of life and standing tall. However, I have discovered an interesting fact. If I am diligent in my daily watering, this vine becomes so full, it cannot hold it in!

I soon begin seeing sparkling drops of water at the tips of each leaf. As I have watched the cycle over the years, God has used it to speak to my heart. This ten-year-old philodendron is a physical reminder of my walk with God. At first, I was daily in the word. I grew and stretched beyond where I was originally planted. God used many around me to help encourage my growth and to make sure I stayed filled with His living water.

As time went on, I allowed the cares of the world to press in. I became too busy to find the daily time to drink in the word, until I was completely parched of it. Conversely, when I do remain in His word daily, I find myself so full, I can't contain it and it pours out of me to everyone around. I still sometimes struggle with staying centered in God's truth, but I find myself looking up more often. It is amazing how God can use anything, even a simple houseplant, to draw you to himself.

So where are you friends? Are you drooping, weary, and dying for a taste of His living water? Are you stretching your roots and growing your leaves? Or are you so full you are simply bursting to share what you have with others? Take time today to fill your cup and drink deep of God's Spirit.

Psalm 42:1 NIV

As the deer pants for the water, so my soul pants for you, O God. My soul thirsts for God, for the Living God.